Contemplation
and
Midlife Crisis

Contemplation *and* Midlife Crisis

EXAMPLES *from* CLASSICAL *and* CONTEMPORARY SPIRITUALITY

Rosemarie Carfagna, OSU

Paulist Press
New York/Mahwah, NJ

Cover and book design by Lynn Else

Copyright © 2008 by Ursuline Academy of Cleveland

All rights reserved. No part of this book may be reproduced or transmitted in any form or by any means, electronic or mechanical, including photocopying, recording, or by any information storage and retrieval system without permission in writing from the Publisher.

Library of Congress Cataloging-in-Publication Data

Carfagna, Rosemarie, 1947–
    Contemplation and midlife crisis : examples from classical and contemporary spirituality / Rosemarie Carfagna.
      p. cm.
    Includes bibliographical references.
    ISBN 978-0-8091-4498-3 (alk. paper)
    1. Middle-aged persons—Religious life. 2. Midlife crisis—Religious aspects—Christianity. 3. Spiritual life—Catholic Church. I. Title.
    BV4579.5.C36 2008
    248.8'4—dc22

                                          2007047256

Published by Paulist Press
997 Macarthur Boulevard
Mahwah, New Jersey 07430

www.paulistpress.com

Printed and bound in the
United States of America

Contents

Introduction vii

Chapter 1 Crisis 1
    Transitions, 1
    Involuntary Change, 5
    Loss, 8
    Impasse, 12
    Trauma, 16
    Desire, 19

Chapter 2 Midlife Crisis 24
    Crisis of Limits, 24
    Crisis of Meaning, 28
    Crisis of Faith, 31
    Emergence of the Self, 35
    Spirit Desires Meaning, 39
    Encounter with the Absolute, 42

Chapter 3 Accompanying States 47
    Depression, 48
    Desolation, 53
    Dark Night, 60
    Similarities and Differences, 66

Chapter 4 Experiential Signs 72
    Loss of Identity, 73
    Irreconcilable Opposites, 76
    Personal Weakness, 78
    Emotional Pain, 80
    Anxiety, 82
    Powerlessness, 83

Dependence, 85
Absence, 88
Emptiness, 90
Abyss, 92
New Life, 94

Chapter 5 Response 96
Choice, 97
Finite Meets Infinite, 100
Divine Initiative, 104
Surrender, 107
Individuation, 110
Union with Jesus, 114

Chapter 6 Contemplation 118
Attending, 119
Recollection, 122
Contemplation, 124
New Knowing, New Loving, 127
Disappearance of the False Self, 129
Centering, 131
Still Point, 134
Indwelling, 137

Chapter 7 Resolution 140
Healing, 141
Humility, 144
Expansion, 146
Beyond Contradictions, 148
Integration, 151
Transformation, 153
True Self, 156
Spiritual Maturity, 159

Notes 163

Bibliography 174

Introduction

This book has been in preparation for some time. As I have been working on it, people have occasionally asked me about the topic. When I tell them that I am writing a book about crisis and contemplation, I get intriguing responses. Some people smile knowingly and proceed no further. Others say that they know a great deal about crisis but nothing about contemplation. What has amazed me, though, is the number of people who identify immediately with the pairing of these two experiences. Without any probing on my part, one woman told me about a health crisis that threatened and eventually deepened her faith. A man I knew only slightly described his emotional paralysis when his business collapsed, and his subsequent experience of radical dependence upon God. However, the most profound recognition of the connection between crisis and contemplation seems to come from people in their middle years. Invariably these are people of good faith who have given selflessly to their families, who have dedicated many years to their professions, and who have been forced by life experiences to renegotiate their relationships with God.

My hope is that an exploration of crisis experiences will suggest possible connections between crisis and contemplative prayer. Personal crisis, especially midlife crisis, has a great deal in common with contemplation. Both focus the individual on the immediate present. Both thrust the individual into the unknown. Both challenge the individual's personal resources, assumptions, and customary ways of proceeding. In drawing out these and other similarities, I would like to provide, for faithful people who are in crisis, a spiritual context that may help them to understand better their experience. I also intend to show that personal crisis may bring them to a quiet form of contemplation, one that simply rests in the presence of God. In fact, I suggest that at certain moments the crisis itself becomes their prayer. In crisis, when we do not know how to pray properly, the Spirit prays within us on our behalf. Not only do crises bring us to our knees, they may also bring us into the very presence of God. For many people, crisis precipitates a degree of intimacy with God they might never have imagined.

In the first part of the book, I describe the phenomenon of crisis from a psychological perspective. For a general description of crisis, I refer to the work of William Bridges, a consultant who had helped numerous businesses cope with corporate crises, and whose own life was turned upside down by his wife's diagnosis with cancer. Philosopher John Crosby and psychiatrist Gerald May expand an understanding of crisis. The personal crisis experiences of poet Kathleen Norris and Episcopal priest Margaret Guenther illustrate the various elements occurring in crises. The life of Augustine gives evidence of his personal crisis of conversion in the early centuries of the Church. Testimonies from Catherine Doherty and Carmelite Constance FitzGerald underline the social implications of unresolved crises.

For an understanding of midlife crisis, I will turn to the work of C. G. Jung, the psychologist who first dealt explicitly with the potential for spiritual deepening in the middle and later years. His ideas, and the life stories of people who will serve as examples of them, will illustrate the complex experiences that may trigger each other simultaneously at midlife: crisis of limits, crisis of meaning, and crisis of faith. Such spiritual greats as Thomas Merton and Henri Nouwen confide that they themselves experienced these things. The encouraging insight gathered from the stories of midlife travelers who have come out the other side of crises is that these somewhat intimidating events frequently act as symptoms of a deeper, more profound emergence of the spirit within. Midlife crises may even announce what British Carmelite Ian Matthew calls the "impact of God" in their lives, a God they are only now ready to meet.

Crisis often generates accompanying emotional states. For those who are familiar with similar but distinctly different accom-

INTRODUCTION

panying experiences, I will make comparisons and contrasts among psychological depression, spiritual desolation, and spiritual dark-night experiences. St. Ignatius offers a sensitive treatment of spiritual desolation and its difference from psychological depression. St. John of the Cross gives a harrowing description of the spiritual dark night, and distinguishes it from depression. Both of these spiritual masters, and the commentators who write in their traditions, serve as invaluable guides in discerning the presence and action of the Spirit in critical times.

People who try to describe what happens to them during a crisis frequently mention experiential signs that contemplatives also report. Figures as ancient as the desert fathers and as contemporary as Cardinal Bernardin of Chicago allude to these signs. In crisis, their sense of identity seems to change. They become aware of apparently irreconcilable opposites. They realize vividly their own weaknesses and shortcomings. Emotions arise that can be very disturbing. There might be feelings of anxiety, even terror of what they find themselves facing. In this turbulent state, they feel powerless to take any meaningful action. They are dependent upon Someone who, at the most critical moment, seems to have abandoned them. The sense of abandonment leaves them feeling starkly alone, teetering on the edge of an abyss, confronting an unknown, impenetrable Absolute as unequivocal as death.

If you have survived the previous paragraph, you will be relieved to hear that at this point things begin to change. The individual is confronted with what C. S. Lewis calls a moment of wholly free choice. The choice is between hope and despair. The person either surrenders to the unseen, unknown Being at work in his or her irreversible circumstances or toys with the option of despair. In the midst of his ambiguous experience, that much is clear. If a person chooses in the affirmative, she makes a profound act of faith. That person makes what Kierkegaard and others have referred to as a blind leap. In making that act of faithful surrender, although immersed in irresolvable difficulties, many faithful people permanently redirect the inner orientation of their lives.

Contemplative experience serves as a map for the uncharted territory that might come next. Key figures from the Christian faith tradition offer insights into their own experience that can assist those in crisis today. An anonymous medieval monk envisions himself suspended before God who hides behind *The Cloud of Unknowing*. Teresa of Avila and John of the Cross describe their invisible experiences using concrete images with which everyone can identify: an inner wine cellar, the rain, a burning log, and an artist's model. These spiritual masters, and the contemporary men and women whose commentaries convey their experiences to us, highlight aspects of contemplation that ring true for the person in crisis. They admit to a form of prayer characterized by urgent desiring, prolonged searching, and patient waiting. They describe letting go of virtually everything, and eventually coming to a still point in the center where they meet God.

Placing the suffering of midlife crisis in relation to the suffering of Jesus unlocks the mystery uniting crisis with contemplative prayer. Julian of Norwich vividly beholds Christ crucified and almost instantaneously envisions Christ risen. She understands that the suffering and resurrection of Christ embrace human suffering and hold hope for risen human life. Margaret Dorgan underlines this insight from the Carmelite tradition and David Lonsdale from the tradition of Ignatius. In their accounts, these commentators and others capture the simultaneity of dying and rising in the Paschal Mystery of Jesus. They propose that the resurrection of Jesus is invisibly available to all faithful people at every moment, especially at moments that are most critical.

The effects of an encounter with God, or with the Absolute an agnostic may prefer to address, are palpable. The first and most universally mentioned effect is an increase in humility, followed closely by an ongoing process of personal purification and deep psychic healing. Consciousness expands, the inner being opens, and a new authentic identity emerges. Contemplatives and those who choose hope rather than despair in times of crisis

INTRODUCTION

are transformed. They see things differently, make sense of apparent contradictions, and love with seemingly inexhaustible love. Numerous classic and contemporary lives reflect these realities. Narratives of midlife travelers show that when individuals choose to resolve personal crises with affirmations of faith, regardless of the outcomes on the material level, they come to a state of real spiritual maturity. They share with contemplatives a sense of the presence of God, within them and around them. God's presence brings peace, an inner peace that the external world cannot give. Like the faithful surrender that leads to it, this peace is solid and unshakable.

My hope is that you will not be so put off by the initial descriptions of crisis, and midlife crisis in particular, that you will turn back and miss the best part of the story. I hope that in recognizing the universality of the experience of crisis, and the possibility of its positive resolution, you will see the hand of the loving God who sustains us through absolutely everything.

1
Crisis

Rather than plunging immediately into the murky waters of midlife, we will begin by looking at the phenomenon of crisis in a more general way. Crises can be as minor as a relocation due to one's work or as major as the premature death of a spouse. Although they are of many and varied kinds, most crises share a few common characteristics. They represent transitions in our lives, they initiate involuntary change, and they are triggered by such uncomfortable experiences as loss, impasse, trauma, or desire. Let us explore each of these characteristics and possible triggers to see whether they serve to build a preliminary understanding of crisis with which to develop a clearer context for the very unique experience of midlife crisis.

Transitions

William Bridges is a business consultant who helps corporations and large organizations cope with the inevitable adjustments they must make. In his capacity as a consultant he developed a theoretical framework to describe change as it affects people and their ability to adapt. His framework suggests that change occurs when one state of affairs ends, throwing us into a vague neutral zone, until a new state of affairs begins and takes hold. The pattern is simple: ending, neutral zone, beginning again.[1] Anyone who has ever relocated can grasp the concept. Even if the relocation is a desirable one, it still necessitates packing, moving, and unpacking. Young executives joke about their wedding presents staying in boxes until their third anniversary because they were too busy to unpack them when they arrived at the new location to advance their careers. I imagine young executives take well to Bridges' scheme.

CONTEMPLATION AND MIDLIFE CRISIS

In the case of personal crisis, however, the pattern is not as clear-cut. The end may be the end of something we highly valued or dearly loved. The neutral zone may keep us in unfamiliarity for an intolerable period of time. Beginning again may seem unpromising or even impossible. It is as if the optimism and energy needed to begin again left us along with all that has ended.

This is the situation in which Bridges found himself. After having successfully guided many other people through seamless transitions in the workplace, he found himself thrown into a transition for which he was totally unprepared. His wife was diagnosed with an advanced stage of cancer that spread rapidly and led to her death. The diagnosis represented the end of their marriage as they had shared it for many years. From then on their combined energies would be directed toward the arduous activities of medical treatment and toward waiting to see whether a possible but unlikely remission might occur. From the moment of her diagnosis, through the months of her treatment and illness, and for several months after her death, Bridges inhabited a shadowy, colorless neutral zone. The unknowns in the situation would not budge. He wondered how long she would be ill and how much she would suffer. He could not picture life without her. What would he do by himself after she was gone?

During the whole time Bridges accompanied his wife through her illness, his world stood still. Strange things happened to his experience of time. Hours in doctors' offices seemed like days, but days passed by far too quickly. In his grief and loss he felt "stripped," "dismantled," "naked."[2] His competent professional consultant personality seemed to have evaporated. He felt unable to have any effect on his wife's illness or on its relentless progression. His wife and their marriage were such essential components of his personality that he felt himself completely adrift without her. He was painfully aware of the major adjustments rebuilding his life would require. He could not even imagine himself attempting them. Recollections of his energetic motivational presentations on the benefits of life transitions haunted him.

Bridges eventually did begin again. The painful ending that precipitated his transition, and the seemingly interminable neutral zone through which he stumbled, brought out unexpected strengths in him. Writing about the experience later, he says that living in the anonymous neutral zone became a spiritual discipline for him. It forced him to draw on inner resources he did not know were there. He developed patient acceptance, a minimum of trust, and an increased ability to live with the ambiguity of life. Ironically, before his wife's diagnosis, they had begun a major renovation of their home. Throughout her illness, they had lived with painters' cloths draped in various places, new electrical wiring hanging exposed, and sheets of drywall leaning against cupboards. As a priority, home improvement paled in comparison with the drama of her struggle. Immediately following his wife's death, the dismantled state of their home seemed symbolic to him of the state of his own life.

However, as his grief diminished and his appetite for life returned, Bridges addressed the home renovation to fill his otherwise empty, amorphous time. To his surprise, the physical tasks involved in remodeling began to represent his new beginning. He threw himself into projects with abandon. Plumbing, tiling, grouting, and painting focused and reoriented him. The completion of each practical task confirmed the fact that he was able to bring things together and make them work. He began to take pride in the appearance of the renovated space. Working on it had tapped into skills that had been latent inside him. Offering his own experience as encouragement to others, he says, "It is as though the breakdown of the old reality releases energy that has been trapped in the form of our old lives and converts it back into its original state of pure and formless energy."[3] The creative energy released when he began to choose life again opened new and unforeseen possibilities for him.

Yet, for many months the formlessness of the energy that returned to Bridges was more threatening than reassuring. He felt ready to begin again, but was unsure how to do that. Should he change careers? Marry again? Move to a new city? The vague nature of the neutral zone frustrated him. Fortunately, he had the good sense to postpone any major decisions until the fog had cleared. Eventually, after a lengthy period of bereavement and personal rebuilding, he did begin again. He brought what he had learned from his own experience of transition into his consulting practice, making it more sensitive and realistic than it had been before. He renewed old friendships and risked making new connections with other people. Confidence returned, and a somewhat sobered optimism. Once again, he began to live.

William Bridges' story serves as an example of the general phenomenon of crisis. In crisis there is a sharp, unavoidable break with the status quo, and there is no immediately apparent alternative that is viable and attractive. The comfort of familiarity disappears, and the unfamiliarity of what lies ahead looms large. Ordinary coping mechanisms weaken and prove ineffective. Questions arise that undermine confidence and threaten the ability to move on. Loss of security sets off a series of reactions including emotional pain, grief, and fear. The more accomplished we are, the more disruptive a life crisis can be. Besides being unprepared for the crisis, we feel unable to deal with it. Logic, efficiency, competence, and the other tools of our pre-crisis life are of no help. Instead, when we try to use them they seem to make matters worse.

Bridges hints at the spiritual potential of crisis. He learned that crisis not only breaks down our defenses but also breaks through former barriers. It calls us to risk, openness, and trust. Within a crisis, he sees a turning point signified by "the willingness to view our own individual crises as critical opportunities to let go of who we have been, and to set forth on the journey toward becoming something more."[4] The "something more" we will become is a more spiritual self, more patient, less proud, more open to mystery, less demanding of certainty. If we can situate personal crisis within the ongoing journey of faith development, we will unlock its full spiritual potential. By its urgency, crisis may move us to act more courageously than ever before. It may free us to walk in blind faith. It is at this very point of blind faith that the experience of the person in crisis most closely resembles that of the one in contemplative prayer. Certainly not all people in crisis are people of faith, nor are they all contemplatives, but for the person of faith, crisis can introduce a more contemplative approach to life.

Involuntary Change

Unwanted transitions can exacerbate a routine life change into a personal crisis. Involuntary change attacks our autonomy, our ability to direct our own lives. As long as we are orchestrating the changes in our lives, we find the flexibility to adapt to them gracefully. The young adult carefully chooses a career path in life and is willing to expend the energy needed to follow it. A married couple decides to forgo an expensive vacation, preferring to use the money they would have spent to pay down an ominous level of debt. An older couple sells their family home and moves to Arizona while they are still healthy enough to enjoy their retirement. In initiating changes, these individuals exercise personal autonomy. They assess their circumstances, review alternatives, consider the pros and cons of each, and make a prudential judgment that best suits their personal goals and desires. Referring to responsible decisions such as these, John Crosby says, "It belongs precisely to the rightly understood autonomy of persons that they have not only their being in themselves, but have as well their worth in themselves."[5] Exercising autonomy in this way reinforces our identity and self-confidence. We feel we are in charge of our lives, and we accept the changes implied by our decisions as part of the price we pay for being responsible, worthwhile people.

A very different scenario unfolds when someone else or some external factor initiates the change. If the externally prompted change disrupts life significantly, we may enter a period of crisis. We may react defensively even when, according to some objective criterion, the change represents an enhancement of our lives. Let us consider the situation in which Carol, a recently married woman, found herself. Shortly after their marriage, Carol's husband accepted a promotion in his company, which necessitated a cross-country move for them. Because the promotion represented a hard-earned reward for her husband and the chance for a better life for their future family, Carol consented to the move. Although she had never lived outside of her hometown and was very close to her aging parents, she agreed to give it a try.

Leaving the east coast and making a home on the west coast created a degree of disturbance in Carol that she did not anticipate. After several months of sincere effort, she was forced to admit her unhappiness with the move, and her fear that she might not be able to adjust. Everything irritated her. The weather was wrong, the food was strange, the people were unfriendly, and she was left alone too much while her husband invested most of his time in the challenges of his new position. She wondered whether she had made a mistake in attempting the move, or even in entering into her marriage. Loneliness, separation from family and friends, drastic differences in local culture, and the natural upheaval of the first year of marriage all took their toll on Carol. She had not asked for this, yet she was forced to deal with it.

Involuntary change undermines our sense of autonomy. Whatever threatens our autonomy also threatens our sense of security and self-worth. In involuntary change, things happen over which we have no control. We fear we are no longer in charge. People and forces outside of us seem to wreak havoc in our lives, and we feel powerless to counteract them. In Carol's case, it was her husband's company that tore her comfortable world apart, but similar dynamics occur in other contexts. A discount chain may decide to open a massive store in a previously idyllic neighborhood. A freak accident may handicap a family member. Economic change may affect a pension fund we had counted on for retirement. These events nullify our plans. Someone or something external to us invades our otherwise smooth-running lives. All of these cases illustrate the menacing power of involuntary change. To a greater or lesser extent, each one could bring someone to a point of personal crisis.

Invasive, unwanted change in our lives exposes a spiritual nerve. It defies the assumption that we know what is best, and that our plans are the only right plans. If we are operating out of ego or pride, we will sustain a severe blow. If we act in humility, we will grow spiritually and discover a deeper level of union with God. Psychiatrist and spiritual director Gerald May describes the spiritual challenge implied in crisis. May says, "It is necessary to walk the fierce path of free will and dependence. We must always claim the freedom we have been given…But at the same time we will increasingly recognize the extreme inadequacy of personal will and knowledge in figuring out what life is or how we should live it."[6] Crisis makes us realize that we are both free and dependent—free to respond to the situations that impact us, but dependent upon God for a panoramic view wide enough to make sense of them. Acknowledging dependence on God gives spiritual weight to the experience of crisis. People of faith turn to God at moments like this, while others may not. Crisis presents us with a choice: rely on our own strength, or surrender to the mysterious power of God at work in our lives.

Involuntary change gives us a chance to look beneath circumstances to God's loving presence hidden within them. We do best to surrender to God, even without seeing clearly how God is present in the circumstances. May calls this a contemplative attitude. He describes a contemplative attitude as "a willingness to appreciate what *is*—just as it is…This attitude is not a devaluation of our knowledge or abilities, but a simple availability of all that we are, just as we are, in the situation just as it is."[7] Perhaps Carol could grow into a contemplative attitude toward her new location. For her, having a contemplative attitude would mean opening her loneliness, doubts, and fears to God without demanding divine intervention to fix herself or her situation. It would mean surrendering in faith to a loving God who is undeniably present both within her and within her situation, however mysteriously that may be. Overlooking the inability to see or feel God's presence in critical moments and surrendering in faith without understanding how God is present deepens our faith and solidifies our dependence on God, the source of our strength.

Crises allow for spiritual growth and deepening. However, seeing crisis as an opportunity for spiritual growth does not imply that God inflicts crises on people or that God wants people to suffer. Rather, discerning the spiritual potential of crisis affirms God's constant presence to people in crisis who are suffering. The affirmation takes the form of being open to God at all times, in all places, regardless of our comfort level or our felt experience of God. An affirming attitude, perhaps discovered in crisis, can become an underlying attitude toward life. May says, "The capacity to experience living moment by moment in God differs among us in matters of degree. Spiritual growth includes an enlargement of this capacity."[8] Living moment by moment in the divine presence unites us with God, the only lasting source of security. The more habitually we remain in God's presence, the better able we are to endure the crises of life.

Loss

In the mid-1970s poet Kathleen Norris and her husband moved from Manhattan to rural South Dakota to manage a family inheritance, a homestead her grandparents had established half a century earlier. Twenty years later Norris recorded her experience of the move and its eventual spiritual benefits for her in the book *Dakota: A Spiritual Biography*. A key element in Norris' adjustment to living on the Great Plains was the issue of loss. She felt she had lost most of what was familiar and comforting for her in the New York literary community. The barrenness of the vast horizon accentuated the absence of taller architecture. Near-empty stores, schools, and churches implied that much of the population had fled. Bus and train service had both left town with the departing people, so that the isolation of the area intensified.

Norris explains that when you first come to the Great Plains, "you have to combat the disorientation and an overwhelming sense of loneliness."[9] Those who are unable to adjust to the immense sky and the high plains desert sometimes succumb to a form of "Plains Fever," which compels them to act impulsively. One guest of hers who could not tolerate the lack of noise and crowds went to a pay phone one night, called a woman he hardly knew, and asked her to marry him. When Norris first moved there, her reaction to the loss of friends and colleagues was even more severe. She admits that realizing all she had given up brought her to a point of desperation. She said, "I'm tempted to despair at times. Dakota can be painfully lonely for an artist."[10]

In her struggle Norris turned inward for spiritual strength. Although she had been away from organized religion for some time, she joined her grandmother's church because it was one of the few social groups active in town. She sang nostalgically from ancient hymnals and read reverently from a battered Bible. Gradually the spirit of her grandmother, who was a deeply religious woman, seemed to stir in her.

Next, partly out of curiosity and partly to escape loneliness, Norris began visiting some hospitable Benedictine monks who lived in a monastery nearby. As she grew to understand their way of life, she became more and more intrigued. She respected the monks' voluntary asceticism, their willingness to do without comforts, and their choice to live largely in silence. The monks taught her that the corollary of the outer space of the Dakota landscape was the inner spiritual space it eventually creates. They showed by their example how one could live in geographic isolation with freedom of heart. She could see that "for one who has chosen the desert and truly embraced the forsaken ground it is not despair or fear of limitation that dictates how one lives. One finds instead an openness and hope that verges on the wild."[11]

The monks' carefree spirit fascinated Norris, because they seemed unperturbed by the extremes of climate and the stark hardships of Plains living. Over the years she became a Benedictine oblate and enjoyed sharing in the liturgy and communal life of the monks. By the time she wrote her spiritual autobiography she could say, "When I look at the losses we've sustained in western Dakota, and at the human cost in terms of anger, distrust and grief, it is the monks and nuns of the Benedictine communities who inspire me to hope."[12] For them and gradually for Norris, what was materially less became spiritually more.

Not everyone who struggles with loss enjoys the spiritual support Norris discovered. In her book *Toward Holy Ground*, Margaret Guenther portrays an even more isolated population than the Plains people. Guenther, an Episcopal priest, ministers to the frail elderly in nursing homes, offering them what spiritual support she can in their greatly reduced circumstances. She describes Klara, an educated woman who came to the nursing home after shattering her hip and never returned to her apartment. Because Klara was a woman of books, her most acute deprivation was the loss of her library, for which there was no room in the nursing home. Guenther says, "She thought about each of her books and mourned them as one might mourn lost friends."[13] Guenther sketches out the cluster of other losses that afflict the frail elderly. They suffer the loss of mobility, greatly narrowing their perspective on the world. They lose their privacy, many of their possessions, and ultimately their "carefully crafted identity."[14] In their decline, they are no longer spouse, attorney, confidante, or boss. They are reduced to the bare minimum, and they hold onto that with a tenuous grip.

With loss comes grief. Guenther learned that grief, when it is allowed to play itself out, can have a liberating effect. She offers the example of the most distressing loss of all, the loss of one's home. Capturing the understandable human reaction of her clients to the loss of their homes, she says, "It did not matter that their new surroundings were clean and bright, that good meals were served in an almost elegant dining room. They grieved for home—broken pipes, cockroaches and falling plaster notwithstanding."[15]

Guenther patiently shared her clients' grief. She listened to their tender stories and respected their need to mourn. Some of her clients could not move beyond grief, but many others did. In those who grew to accept their losses, Guenther saw real spiritual gains.

Among the fruits of loss Guenther witnessed in her clients was a simplification of life. Having little, they finally needed little. Priorities shifted and changed. Stripped of everything superficial, they became comfortable living with bare essentials. If their minds were still functioning well, they could provide real wisdom. Guenther says, "The very old and the very sick who are able to embrace loss and live through desolation are often willing, even eager to deal with the issues of deep meaning."[16] The trick is in learning to embrace loss and to endure its stripping power. As often happens in ministry, Guenther learned life lessons from those she served. The beauty and freedom of acceptance in the frailest elderly showed a degree of spiritual depth she desired to attain herself.

Painful as they are, losses can open spiritual space in us. The decisive issue in whether they do so or not is our response to them. By their very nature losses threaten and disquiet us. We are inclined to rebel against them. If we invest our energy in resisting them, some losses will deepen and inflict more emotional harm. But if we can tolerate inevitable diminishments, we may find life simpler and its difficulties easier to bear. The difference is in our consciously chosen priorities and in our inner orientation. Enduring material loss leaves us more appreciative of the immaterial values of the spirit. Such qualities as courage, trust, authenticity, and acceptance are rooted in the spirit and cannot be taken from us by external forces.

The frail elderly exemplify the ideal presented by St. Paul, who said, "We do not lose heart. Even though our outer nature is wasting away, our inner nature is being renewed day by day."[17] It is the inner being that endures the losses of life and makes of them opportunities for spiritual deepening. It is the spirit that emerges strengthened from experiences of desperation. If we remain faithful through periods of acute deprivation, we will realize true spiritual gains. We will feel and act differently, having accepted life's inevitable pains. May Norris' monks and Guenther's elderly be models for us in accepting the losses in our own lives. May we experience the spiritual freedom they enjoy.

Impasse

On the very eve of the Russian revolution, the Baroness Catherine de Hueck and her husband Boris escaped from Russia through Finland and later made their way to Canada. They brought little with them and nearly were destitute shortly after their arrival. Catherine turned to fervent prayer for strength, and to the reading of Scripture. "One day her eyes fell on the Scripture passage, 'Go, sell what you own and give the money to the poor, and you will have treasure in heaven; then come, follow me.'"[18] Those words announced a unique call that would inspire Catherine to dedicate herself to God and compel her to work with the poor and marginalized for the rest of her life. She went on to found Madonna House, a lay apostolic movement rooted in contemplative prayer. When she died in 1985, Madonna House had more than two hundred staff workers and field houses on five continents.[19]

Between the scriptural call received in Montreal in 1929 and her death as a beloved foundress in 1985, Catherine met every conceivable sort of obstacle and indignation. Working with and for the poor, and speaking out boldly on their behalf, put her on the firing line continually. She lived in Harlem in 1939, and shared with the poor the impact of destitution and despair. When she tried to call attention to the deplorable conditions of the African American people in Harlem, she encountered the problem of racism firsthand. She says, "Although my faith was strong, for maybe a year or so I underwent an agony, a temptation that is very hard to describe. The temptation came from seeing the evil done by people in the U.S. to the Negro and other minorities while mouthing the Gospel. This is hypocrisy.

Where is God in it all?"[20] The collective prejudices and discriminations that impacted the African Americans in Harlem in the late 1930s built a wall Catherine could not penetrate. The more vigorous her efforts, the more bitter her frustration. She confronted the devastating effects of social sin.

Catherine's genuine love for the poor and her missionary zeal in advocating for them had brought her to what Carmelite Constance FitzGerald calls an *impasse*. FitzGerald says, "By impasse, I mean that there is no way out of, no way around, no rational escape from, what imprisons one, no possibilities in the situation."[21] She applies the notion of impasse to such human miseries as war and poverty, injustice and oppression. In each of these cases, social forces beyond our control seem to conspire destructively. Even those who are most sensitive to the issues are stymied. "The temptation to quit, to walk away, becomes overpowering."[22] Catherine de Hueck suffered the poignant power of that temptation herself.

The revolution in Russia, stark poverty in Montreal, her husband's marital infidelities—none of these blows hit Catherine as hard as the reactions to her public condemnations of racism. She says, "Yet always the Spirit urged me on and gave me courage. You have to preach the Gospel without compromise or shut up. One or the other. I tried to preach it without compromise…That's when the rotten eggs and tomatoes would start to fly."[23] Although she appeared to be dauntless, Catherine paid a high price for preaching the social Gospel. She sank into deep discouragement, even despair, and more than once considered suicide. The intractability of the collective conscience infuriated her. The fact that even church leaders did so little to correct the situation thrust her into an ongoing crisis of faith.

FitzGerald could be describing Catherine's experience when she says that encountering impasse generates feelings of powerlessness, hopelessness, and helplessness. These feelings plagued Catherine, as well as a frightening sense of alienation and personal danger. In Savannah, Georgia, when she was speaking to a Catholic women's group at the invitation of the bishop, the audience attacked Catherine physically. The angry women rushed the stage. Years later Catherine remembered the event. She recalled, "My blouse was in shreds, and I was black and blue from the blows of the women."[24] Such violent reactions surely challenged her moral courage, as well as threatening her religious faith. More than once she experienced what St. John of the Cross calls a spiritual dark night.

Constance FitzGerald draws strong correlations between the experience of societal impasse and spiritual dark night. Both phenomena drive the individual to a point near despair. However, while societal impasse remains impenetrable, the spiritual dark night offers one sure strategy for survival. John of the Cross counsels the individual undergoing the dark night to make an act of faith in the midst of darkness. The act of faith may take the form of surrender to God in a moment of apparent failure. Surrender may pose a terrifying risk, but the alternative leaves the individual without any recourse. FitzGerald says, "The person caught in impasse must find a way to identify, face, live with and express this suffering. If one cannot speak about one's affliction in anguish, anger, pain, lament—at least to God within—one will be destroyed by it or swallowed up by apathy."[25] Time and again Catherine brought her anguish to God. She remained faithful to God and to her unique vocation. The personal cost to her was great, but she acquiesced.

Occasionally even seemingly frozen impasses do begin to thaw. Catherine lived to see the success of the Civil Rights movement in the United States, with its legal attempts to address the worst offenses of racism. She also founded and nurtured her life's work, the lay association called Madonna House. As the association's outreach spread and Catherine's popularity grew, she turned more and more frequently to prayer. She who had always been a frenzy of activity became increasingly contemplative. Visitors to Madonna House recognized her as a woman of great faith and deep prayer. They admired her perseverance over the decades and her complete reliance on God. She gave all of the credit to God, and advised staff members and visitors alike to make silent prayer their first priority, even before charitable works.

In her book *Poustinia*, Catherine reminisced about a contemplative tradition in her native Russia. She describes a *poustinia*, a small cabin or room to which one retreats to pray. Saintly souls in Russia would enter the small room for a twenty-four-hour period of contemplative prayer and fasting. They would take only the Scriptures with them, a little bread, and the makings for tea. For the time they were there, they would offer their prayer for the needs of the world. They would commune with God, and ask for God's direction in the active life they would resume when their time of prayer ended. Often, when they returned to their families and friends after having been in the poustinia, they would offer a word of encouragement that they had received there. The word received from God was always hopeful and confident, regardless of how virulent the social problems that they presented were.

In Combermere, Ontario, where Catherine established the headquarters for Madonna House, she built several poustinias in the woods. She invited people of prayer to go there for times of retreat, provided that they included in their prayer the needs of the world. The usual format for poustinia prayer was to be one day of prayer, followed by a number of days of work, and then a possible return to prayer. Prayer was never to be separated from labor, and the individual was never to be separated from the community. Catherine taught that the poor and marginalized, and the societal impasses that entrap them, require constant prayer.

Contemplative prayer had saved Catherine's faith as well as her life. In her later years she would confide to her closest friends how often she felt she was at her absolute limit. Regardless of how critical the limit was or how acute its impact on her, she turned again and again to God for help. She received the success of Madonna House and her own times of contemplative prayer as gifts from God. May her humble witness continue to inspire many others to preach and to live the Gospel without compromise, as she did.

Trauma

The story of Ignatius of Loyola, the sixteenth-century founder of the Jesuits, exemplifies the kind of life crisis that can be brought about by trauma. In his youth Ignatius embodied the stereotype of the courageous, courtly Spanish *hidalgo*, or knight. He was blessed with a fine mind, a good education, and the social skills that come from being raised among the nobility. Growing up, Ignatius internalized the complex ideal of the indomitable warrior and the sophisticated gentleman. He resolved to fulfill the ideal to the highest degree. As a young man, he learned the arts of war, elevating his naturally aggressive temperament to the status of a powerful military commander. His opportunity for glory came in his late twenties, when he led the Spanish troops in a life-or-death struggle against the French in a crucial battle at Pamplona. Under Ignatius' leadership the Spanish defended the garrison valiantly until the French soldiers and artillery breached the walls. "In this moment of high drama…Inigo's personality reached its climactic crescendo—and with the impact of a well-aimed cannonball, came crashing down into ignominious defeat."[26]

By shattering one of his legs and injuring the other, the fateful cannonball not only struck down Ignatius physically, it also crushed his military and courtly ambitions. Physical trauma initiated psychological trauma and brought the development of Ignatius' seemingly limitless potential to an abrupt halt. Wounded, weakened, disarmed, and defeated, he returned to his home at Loyola to ponder the future direction of his life. The time required for painful physical rehabilitation allowed space for honest spiritual reflection. As his body fought for health, his spirit groped for God. His "Rules for the Discernment of Spirits" and the outlines of his profound "Spiritual Exercises" took shape during this period. Through these great written works, the world still reaps the spiritual benefits of Ignatius' dreadful ordeal.

Today sensitivity to worldwide events makes us all too aware of trauma. Besides hearing about traumatic crimes and accidents occurring locally, we see the damaging effects of terrorism, war, and natural disasters everywhere. The attacks on the World Trade Center in 2001 irreversibly changed American history. The tsunami in southern Asia in the last days of 2004 wiped out villages and reshaped coastlines, leaving countless people homeless and claiming the lives of many thousands of known and unknown victims. Reports of suicide bombers in the Middle East have become almost routine. Ironically, with repetition trauma loses its ability to shock. Psychologists tell us that trauma leaves individuals in a static state. They are frozen in the time of the trauma, unable to think or act purposefully and unable to feel anything emotionally. Doctors may save the lives of the injured, and families may bury the bodies of the dead, but the personal tragedies accompanying trauma require many years to heal. It is for that reason that the story of Ignatius of Loyola serves as such a hopeful model for a world too familiar with trauma.

Jesuit psychiatrist W. W. Meissner, SJ, analyzes Ignatius' response to trauma and traces its spiritual consequences. He says, "At Loyola, under the psychic pressures of his traumatic crisis, Inigo became aware of another dimension of reality, the spiritual dimension, which emerged with new vitality and meaning during his convalescence."[27] Many varied dynamics operated in Ignatius' religious conversion. Most significantly, his spiritual response to trauma produced a total transformation of his personality. Over a period of time the fierce warrior morphed into a humble beggar. Under the influence of the Spirit of God, Ignatius freely forfeited the glorified self-images that had previously dominated his life. Prayer and penance replaced status and power as his guiding values. He retreated to a quiet cave at Manresa to listen to God and to ask God to redirect his life.

Meissner notes, "As the conversion process continued, the emerging resolution allowed for shaping of a new identity, now cast specifically in religious and spiritual terms."[28] At the heart of Ignatius' conversion was an ongoing act of surrender to God, a surrender to an unknown future and to God's mysterious plans. Similarly, Ignatian spirituality is characterized by a detached openness to God's loving presence discerned through the interior movements in one's life. As soon as a movement is identified as coming from God, usually through an experience Ignatius calls *consolation*, the individual endeavors to align his will with the will of God suggested by the spiritual inclination. When an interior movement is perceived as drawing one away from God, usually through an experience Ignatius calls *desolation*, the individual strives to reject it. This pattern repeats itself as the person walks in faith, without a clear specification of further steps.

Surrender to God became the underlying theme of Ignatius' life. Hope, peace, and unwavering confidence in God led him forward. Energies he had previously invested in worldly pursuits he now dedicated to the works of God. In Ignatius, as in others like him, "the conversion experience represents a process of growth toward greater personal and spiritual maturity."[29] Soon others were drawn to follow him, and the Society of Jesus took on its initial shape. Over the centuries the Jesuits, a group of dedicated men formed in the spirit of surrender to God, would assume worldwide influence. Their stature and accomplishments would far surpass Ignatius' youthful hopes of becoming a favorite at court or a success on the battlefield. The cannonball launched at Pamplona sparked a conversion in Ignatius that became a spiritual movement still active throughout the Church.

Of course the story of Ignatius casts the experience of trauma in the best possible light. Realistic people know that life traumas resolve themselves positively only with personal effort, professional help, and supernatural grace. A trauma less glamorous than Ignatius' can impede personal growth and waylay constructive plans for one's life. A high school football injury can negate hopes for a college scholarship. An armed robbery can terrify homeowners so that they feel unsafe in their most intimate space. Domestic violence can traumatize the children who witness it and undercut their prospects for peaceful family life in the future. We need to acknowledge the crippling effects of cases such as these.

Survivors of trauma are rudely exposed to events outside of the ordinary. They lack a context for understanding the tragedies that beset them. Without warning, traumatic events alter the trajectory of their life plans. These events stun, they numb, they stop people in their tracks. Ordinary consciousness cannot absorb the implications of serious trauma. Survivors who hope to make sense of their disrupted lives must move beyond ordinary consciousness to find meaning and direction for the future. One way to do that is to turn to the spiritual dimension, as Ignatius did. The spiritual dimension will not repair traumatic damage nor erase painful memories, but it can bring survivors into the presence of God, the only source of deep healing. Nor does spiritual healing happen immediately. Healing, if it comes at all, takes time, patience, and a willingness to trust God even after experiencing deeply disturbing events.

Thus far we have dealt mostly with the difficult side of crisis, evidenced in painful transitions, involuntary change, loss, impasse, and trauma. In the next section we will turn to the more positive side of crisis: the breakthrough of desire, a desire that makes business as usual impossible. In ardent desire, the spirit moves. It refuses to settle for the status quo; it presses impatiently for more. The only "more" that will satisfy it is the love of God, manifest in every sort of life experience, however mysteriously that may be.

Desire

When Gerald May was nine years old, his father died. Decades later May confessed that his father's death created a void in his life that was intolerable for him as a nine-year-old boy. Finding no human explanation of the death that satisfied him, May blamed God. Previously he had had a comfortable relationship with God, a simple childlike faith. After his father's death, he says, "something hurt and angry in me, something deeper than my consciousness, chose to dispense with God. I would take care of myself; I would go it alone."[30] May's defiant declaration of independence from God carried him through the study of literature and philosophy in college and the study of science in medical school. When he began his psychiatric practice, however, May realized that he needed more than science to help the troubled patients he treated.

May's work with people addicted to narcotics and alcohol offered an unexpected opportunity for his return to belief in God. Among the people with whom he worked, he recognized that those who were recovering well from their addictions did so because they acknowledged a power greater than themselves. He explains, "They didn't all use religious terms, but there was no doubt in my mind that what they spoke of was spiritual. Something about what they said reminded me of home. It had something to do with turning to God."[31] Associating with grateful, humble, recovering addicts rekindled May's long suppressed desire for God. When it returned, his desire "seemed to pick up where it left off some twenty years earlier…and I gradually became able to reclaim it as my true heart's desire, and the most precious thing in my life."[32]

Desire can powerfully orient one's life. It can inspire, but it can also disturb. Unsatisfied desire can frustrate and discourage, precisely because it demands satisfaction so adamantly. A prime example of a man driven by desire is the illustrious Augustine of Hippo, bishop of the early Church, who recorded his youthful exploits in his autobiographical *Confessions*. *Confessions* reveals that strong physical appetites and a penetrating intellect dominated Augustine's early life. Ambition quickly catapulted him from being a poorly paid tutor of North African schoolboys to writing speeches for the Emperor in Rome and then to holding the coveted Chair of Rhetoric at the University of Milan, all the while living a life of unbridled self-indulgence and bitter dissatisfaction. In his book, *The Darkness of God*, Denys Turner suggests the underlying impetus behind Augustine's insatiable desire, and its numerous frustrating disappointments. Turner says, "In every human desire there is some echo, however faint, of God who, in every human desire is in some way desired."[33]

Augustine's ambitions hid a desire for God, without his consciously perceiving it.

It was not until Augustine met Ambrose, Bishop of Milan, that his heart attained any rest. Augustine saw in Ambrose a man of faith and integrity, at peace with himself and with God. Immediately, he felt drawn to become the sort of person Ambrose was. He presented himself to Ambrose as a proud but desperate man, in need of something or someone that would satisfy him. He sought Christian instruction from Ambrose, and in due course baptism. During his prolonged catechesis, Augustine battled his desires mightily, only to discover an intense need to go beyond himself before he would find the peace he saw in Ambrose. In his ongoing combat with desire Augustine personified the struggle of Paul, who said, "I do not understand my own actions. For I do not do what I want, but I do the very thing I hate."[34] Conversion and reformation of life came slowly for him.

Theologian Walter Conn situates the ongoing struggle between desire and frustration in our basic human nature. Conn says, "Every person has a radical desire to reach out, to move beyond, and to transcend the self…This radical desire for self-transcendence is at the source of everything that is specifically human."[35] The desire for self-transcendence arises out of our felt need to go beyond our own limitations. In honest moments our inadequacies reproach us. We realize that in ourselves we have neither the intellect, nor the skill, nor the competence to handle most of what life delivers to us. Left to our own devices, we are liable to fail and disappoint. Self-transcendence does not erase such human deficits; it simply goes beyond them. The impulse to transcend ourselves and our obvious weaknesses sends us urgently searching for more.

The desire for self-transcendence explains universal experiences like the thirst for knowledge, the motivation to excel, the courage to set goals, and the risk of love. Each of these movements pulls us out of ourselves toward something or someone beyond us. It is part of our makeup to desire to be more than we are already, however unsettling that desire may be. Desiring to know and love

God, who is infinitely greater than we are, profoundly motivates our lives, whether we realize it or not. Authentic hope, personal development, and spiritual maturity spring from that desire.

Gerald May, for example, became acutely aware of his limitations as a psychiatrist and readily admitted his need to transcend his own abilities if he was to be of real help to his patients. May found in God the only source of love and goodness that would satisfy him and that could help him to heal the deep dissatisfaction he encountered in others. As a veteran practitioner he says, "After twenty years of listening to the yearnings of people's hearts, I am convinced that all human beings have an inborn desire for God...It is a longing for love. It is a hunger to love and be loved, and to move closer to the Source of love."[36] How humbling it is to discover that all humans bear within them an insatiable longing for love.

Augustine also came to this admission, although circuitously. In the arrogance of his youth, deep longing expressed itself as a search for himself. He reached greedily for the familiar goals of power, acquisition, and pleasure, only to find them poorly lacking and himself impoverished by his pursuit of them. The more intense his desire for proposed rewards, the more bitter his disappointment in winning them. None of them affirmed him in his innermost being where his need was most pressing. In desperation, Augustine redirected his search for himself into a search for God, and in doing so learned that the two were united. Turner says, "Augustine came to see that these two pursuits, the search for God and the search for himself, were in fact the same search; that to find God was possible only in and through the discovery of the self, and that the self was discoverable only where God was to be found."[37]

Although more than a millennium separates May from Augustine, their common desire to transcend the self and to search for God appears to be the same. Their stories awaken our own desires, known and unknown. They inspire us to continue to reach out, to search, to risk, and to trust, or to begin again if we have given up. They illustrate the fact that in their deepest nature, our desires bring us closer to God. We may go through twenty years of unbelief, as May did, or through an aching process of conversion as Augustine did, but God who is eternal remains. Approaching God may require personal transformations we would rather avoid. Nevertheless, the spirit within us makes such transformations possible. God who is infinitely beyond us uses our desires to draw our yearning spirits further. Our role is to cooperate with the process.

2
Midlife Crisis

Perhaps the most thoroughly documented example of the phenomenon of crisis is the one many people experience at midlife. At this time, harsh realities of life dull people's idealism. Their employers treat them unfairly, their children mystify them, and the energy and optimism of their youth gradually wane. Even the fortunate ones who have achieved a measure of success, popularity, and security by midlife are vulnerable to this experience. Suddenly, everything seems stale.

Multiple factors may converge during the mysterious period called midlife. Often midlifers meet a crisis of limits, a realization that they can go no further in terms of optimal health, career advancement, or family matters. This experience may throw these individuals into a crisis of meaning, a time of questioning the value and worth of their whole past lives. In some cases, especially for faithful people, the crisis of meaning may evolve into a crisis of faith. They may wonder whether God has misled them, whether God cares about them, whether God is even real for them at this crucial time. This chapter will begin to explore the mystery of midlife and the spiritual implications for those immersed in it. It will trace the emergence of a more spiritual self in the midlife journey, one that seeks deeper meaning and brings a person to an encounter with the Absolute that mirrors the experience of contemplation.

Crisis of Limits

At age fifty-four Henri Nouwen, the well-known Dutch priest, teacher, author, and spiritual friend to countless people, made an abrupt change in the direction of his life. Previously, at the acclaimed Menninger Institute, he had been a pioneer in the field of spiritual psychology. Over the years, students at some of the nation's most prestigious universities—Notre Dame, Yale, and Harvard—had packed his courses. People who desired spiritual guidance and growth had eagerly sought his books. Invitations for speaking engagements had multiplied exponentially. Yet, biographer Michael Ford tells us, "Within the confines of the academic structure, Nouwen felt frustrated, lonely and unappreciated."[1] Literally, he felt he could not go on. He had reached the pinnacle of the academic life, and he was acutely dissatisfied. His spirit would give him no rest.

Nouwen typifies someone experiencing a crisis of limits. Having reached the outer limits of a variety of measurable criteria for success and happiness, he was utterly miserable inside. Midlife brings many gifted, dedicated, accomplished people to this point. Clergyman Robert Stoudt captures the scenario vividly. He says, "It is precisely at this point in life, at what appears to be a zenith of sorts that the inexplicable occurs. At the height of one's acknowledged energy, talents and achievements, the bottom seems to drop out…suddenly…a trap door opens unceremoniously under one's feet."[2] Where does one go from there?

As many readers of this book may know, it was at this point in his life that Nouwen chose to leave academic and public life completely. He chose to live and work at Daybreak, a home for the mentally and physically handicapped in Ontario, Canada, that was part of the international L'Arche community founded by Jean Vanier. There, ministering to the daily physical needs of a severely handicapped boy named Adam brought Nouwen to the extreme opposite end of the spectrum from the esoteric academic milieu. Admittedly clumsy and inept, Nouwen gradually learned to dress, feed, and bathe Adam, who was totally incapable of caring for himself. In these humble, physical tasks of ordinary life, Nouwen's spirit soared. It was as if his drastic course correction had finally brought him home.

Psychologist Michael Gerzon offers a metaphor for midlifers who undertake such directional changes. Gerzon says, "In the second half of life, our old compasses no longer work. The magnetic fields alter. The new compass that we need cannot be held in our hand, only in our heart. We read it not with our mind alone, but with our soul."[3] Gerzon echoes the thoughts of many other Jungian writers who maintain that the midlife crisis is essentially spiritual in nature. They suggest that midlife impacts many people as a crisis of limits in their physical, psychological, social, and professional lives. Suddenly, they realize that they are no longer young. Each morning seems to bring another physical sign of aging. Long-term friendships change or end. The workplace pushes them to and beyond their level of endurance. Family tensions adamantly resist resolution. These and a whole host of other phenomena herald an impending crisis of limits for which there is no apparent practical remedy.

Perilous warnings notwithstanding, the crisis of limits conceals an elusive gift: a chance to stand still and reassess our lives. Because limits impede us from going further, we are, at least for the moment, stuck in place. This implacable interruption in our progress allows long suppressed questions to emerge. Another part of us senses what lies ahead. It is the spirit, and it will not wait. Midlife commentator James Hollis says, "When one is stunned into consciousness, a vertical dimension, *kairos*, intersects the horizontal plane of life; one's lifespan is rendered in depth perspective: 'Who am I, then, and whither bound?'"[4] Even faint traces of a path that will feed the spirit draw us irresistibly forward.

Such was the case for Henri Nouwen. His move from Harvard University to the L'Arche community at Daybreak demonstrated an earnest response to a deeper call. Having inspired students, readers, audiences, and friends, he now needed to follow his own inspiration, whether or not others understood or accepted his actions. "Many people admired his decision, at the age of fifty-four, to abandon the prestige of an upwardly mobile life for the unglamorous future of downward mobility, but some of his friends seriously questioned whether Nouwen was doing the right thing."[5] Nouwen's friends' concerns for him were completely legitimate. Practically speaking, the move made no sense.

In inexplicable ways, the joyful simplicity of the L'Arche community gradually healed Nouwen's troubled soul. Inarticulate youngsters cheerfully surrounded this man of well-crafted words. Menial household duties counteracted years of abstract thinking. The unpretentious bonds of camaraderie among the handicapped residents and their kindly assistants constituted an open, welcoming community Nouwen had always longed for but had never previously found. His spirit responded gracefully. As theologian John Sachs says, "Grace is experienced in those 'limit situations' when, faced with Mystery which evades all our attempts to understand life's paradoxes and contradictions, we embrace it gratefully in its joys and sorrows, hopes and despairs."[6]

If limit situations bring us face-to-face with Mystery, they may also place us in the position often assumed by contemplatives. Contemplatives accept the presence of Mystery without being able to understand or explain it. Contemplation remains present to Mystery without thinking or feeling anything specific. Midlifers in limit situations stand still by default; they cannot do otherwise. Contemplatives do so by choice; they desire to remain there. Midlifers and contemplatives share the experience of being present to Mystery, although they do so in different ways. Both may either embrace or resist the encounter. Midlifers tempted to resist may look to contemplatives for a better option. Embracing Mystery deepens our involvement with God, invisibly present in limit situations. We cannot even explain to others what it is that we embrace. More peaceful acceptance of our limits may be the only outward clue.

By walking away from academic life when he had reached its peak, Nouwen broke through external limits and discovered an unexpected spiritual realm within. His choice exemplifies the choices many people must make when midlife brings them to limits they feel they cannot pass. At this difficult and distressing time some, like Nouwen, let the spirit lead them. Others struggle continuously or choose badly. Those who sustain a crisis of limits for an extended period of time may wonder how and why they hang on. They may enter a crisis of meaning that further challenges the smug complaisance of the first half of life.

Crisis of Meaning

Fifteen years into his marriage, Russian writer Leon Tolstoy began to question the value of his life and work. He had a good, loving wife; healthy, rambunctious children; a large, prosperous estate; and a well-established reputation as a scholar and author. He was physically strong and, by his own report, could keep up with any peasant mowing in the fields. He could sustain mental work for eight to ten hours at a stretch. However, even as he acknowledged these enviable conditions, Tolstoy began to regard them as insufficient and subtly lacking. Having lived a nearly flawless life up to that point, he felt that he had somehow lost his way. In his "Confession" he wrote, "Five years ago, a strange state of mind began to grow upon me: I had moments of perplexity...as if I did not know how I was to live, what I was to do, and I began to wander."[7]

Midlife often generates a state of perplexity and a tendency to wander. Midlifers wander beyond the security of the recognizable markers of the first half of life: completing an education, finding one's career, entering into marriage, establishing a home and family. Passing these markers with understandable pride leaves many people looking for the next, less tangible series of markers. They search for the meaning beyond and beneath their apparently charmed, successful lives. They crave a sense of purpose and of further direction, but the further direction points to uncharted territory. A persistent, haunting "why?" prevents them from truly enjoying the comfortable life they already have.

Tolstoy expressed his own search for meaning in stark terms. He wrote, "Before occupying myself with my Samara estate, with the education of my son, with the writing of books, I was bound to know why I did these things. As long as I did not know the reason 'why' I could not do anything, I could not live."[8] Of course, Tolstoy went on to live for many more years, but at the time that he wrote his troubling "Confession," the path to the future seemed barred to him. "I felt that the ground on which I stood was crumbling, that there was nothing for me to stand on, that what I had been living for was nothing, that I had no reason for living…My life had come to a stop…The truth was, that life was meaningless."[9]

Tolstoy's desperation underlines the pressing need all of us have to find meaning in our lives. But because meaning is not an object and cannot be acquired, the search for it is often depicted as an ongoing process or journey. Only the most intrepid travelers willingly undertake a journey with no specific destination, yet that is what the midlife journey entails. Something within us impels us to go further, but where and why, we do not know. One woman we will call Marge described her own chilling moment of reckoning: "There I was. I had a good education, a perfect husband, perfect children, a solid credit rating, a fine neighborhood, and I could not understand why I was so unhappy."

In Marge's case, the problem was profoundly spiritual. Although she had been raised in a devout Catholic home, she had rejected the faith during her college years and had maintained a strict distance from God and the Church ever since. She had provided for some minimal religious education for her children, but Marge had suspended her own relationship with God. Other more objective goals served as her standards: helping her children excel at school and in sports, maintaining a warm and welcoming home, assisting her husband as he advanced in his career. What could possibly be wrong with all this? It was not guilt that troubled her now; it was need. Without fully realizing it, she needed the faith perspective that had guided her youth. Now a responsible adult, she yearned for a mature faith that matched her years.

Marge's story illustrates the spiritual nature of the midlife search for meaning. Addressing this issue, Jungian psychologist

James Hollis says, "There is a hungering energy in the organism, an energy historically identified as spirit, a desire for meaning which the ancients called soul, and a constant, internally corrective system carrying forth the project of spirit and soul, which Jung called the Self."[10] Jung's "Self" is a spiritual impulse within us, moving us toward immaterial goals. It operates in transcendent modes, frequently by process of elimination. As we make fumbling attempts to achieve meaning, the inner Self murmurs, "not this, nor that, nor that." The striving, achieving self of the first half of life would never recognize the carefully discriminating Self of midlife.

Perhaps the Self that emerges at midlife is wiser, more experienced than the earlier self. It may have penetrated layers of superficiality and falsity previously denied. Marge, for example, may finally have realized that the perfection of her life was largely an illusion. Admitting that fact could bring her closer to reality and could allow her to claim a more authentic life from that point on. Hollis explains, "The second adulthood is launched when one's projections have dissolved. The sense of betrayal, of failed expectations, the vacuum and loss of meaning that occur with this dissolution, creates the midlife crisis. It is in this crisis, however, that one has the chance to become an individual."[11]

Becoming an individual who lets the spirit lead initiates a fearsome process of personal metamorphosis. If midlifers relinquish the comfort and security of the first half of life, they may discover to their chagrin the radical openness that the second half of life offers. A slightly cynical *"now what?"* attitude stalks them. Although the realization of radical openness may eventually liberate them, it may at first frighten them, a reaction spiritual director David Lonsdale observes in many of the people he guides. Lonsdale describes the experience of sincere searchers who want to begin all over again in the second half of life. He says, "Even their sense of themselves and of their own worth, which may have been very firm or which they may have struggled to attain, appears to have evaporated, so that they and their world seem to be fragmenting and disintegrating."[12] If someone of the stature of Leon Tolstoy can consider his life's work to be "nothing" and "meaningless," how much more could the ordinary midlife person be tempted to do so?

At the psychological level, nothing could be more threatening for a responsible adult than sensing that all they have accomplished, all they have made of themselves, might be unimportant or even irrelevant. The midlife executive who has risen in business only to learn that he has endangered his health asks, "For *what?*" The midlife woman who intensely guards her independence only to find herself utterly lonely asks, "What went wrong?" These piercing questions catch the persons who ask them and stop them in their tracks. Before proceeding further, they must answer the telling question, "What does it profit them if they gain the whole world, but lose or forfeit themselves?"[13] The answer to this question, like the midlife crisis itself, is essentially spiritual in nature.

It may be for the better that the old self dies so that a new Self may be born; but the person undergoing the process registers only disorientation. "People who have lived for many years in faith and hope now seem to find themselves adrift on a sea of meaninglessness and desperation; indeed many feel that they no longer have faith and their hope seems very fragile."[14] Lonsdale's compassionate portrayal of midlife searchers he has known suggests the third aspect of midlife crisis that some people endure: a crisis of faith. For a few people, the crisis of limits becomes a crisis of meaning, which in turn becomes a crisis of faith.

Crisis of Faith

Eugene Peterson is a respected Episcopal pastor, author, and educator. When he was in his sixties, he reflected back on a particularly trying time in his personal life and in his pastoral ministry. He tells us, "In my thirtieth year, and four years into my ordination, an abyss opened up before me, a gaping crevasse it was. I had been traveling along a path of personal faith in Jesus

Christ since childhood. In adulthood and entering my life work, the path widened into…a vocation to Gospel ministry…I and my work converged: my work was an extension of my faith."[15] For Peterson, as for many others, the years of early adulthood had been blessed with gratifying feelings of accomplishment and integration. He had immersed himself so totally in his ministry that his faith was inseparable from his work.

"Then this chasm opened up, this split between personal faith and pastoral vocation. I was stopped in my tracks. I looked around for a bridge, a rope, a tree to lay across the crevasse and allow passage. I read books, I attended workshops, I arranged consultations. Nothing worked."[16] Peterson, by now an established leader of a faith community, found himself in a full-blown crisis of faith. The seamless coherence between his work and his faith ripped apart. His people seemed cold and unresponsive. Suddenly, the pastoral work that had so inspired him changed into drudgery. Three times he asked for and received a change of assignment, and three times his dissatisfaction returned. "Each time, I came to a place where I didn't think I could last another week. I was bored. I was depressed…spiritually I was in a bog."[17]

Difficult as it was, Peterson's experience is not uncommon. A businessman we will call Tom went through a similar narrow passage. Although not a clergyman, Tom strongly identified with his parish. He served as lector, Eucharistic minister, and sponsor in the RCIA program. He was a good husband and father, and he worked conscientiously at his job. However, for several years Tom had watched his widowed mother withdraw further and further into the remote world of Alzheimer's disease. As her condition worsened, Tom's anxiety about her welfare increased. He felt pangs of grief when she no longer recognized her grandchildren, and anger at God over the fact that she had to suffer.

When Tom brought his situation to prayer, God seemed to turn a deaf ear. Why did his mother, who had lived such a kindly, generous life, have to spend her final years in this debilitated state? How could a loving God allow such prolonged suffering? Why was he denied the comfort of her caring presence, her wise counsel? How could God take her spirit, and leave her body? Carmelite Margaret Dorgan comments on prayer at times like these. She says, "Of all human experience, pain and loss in their devastating diminishment can make us doubt the merciful love of our creator. Why, why, why rises in our throats. We feel ourselves trapped in our agony."[18] With no relief in sight, we are tempted to give up. Why believe in God, if God seems so aloof? Spiritually, we are very vulnerable. At worst, "demonic voices incite us to doubt."[19]

In his book, *Crisis of Faith, Crisis of Love*, Trappist monk Thomas Keating offers a word of encouragement for those experiencing a crisis of faith. Keating uses numerous biblical examples of figures that grew from spiritual childhood or adolescence to greater spiritual maturity by going through a crisis of faith. The prime challenge to their faith was the death of Jesus. After his ignominious death, how could they believe in him? Until they saw evidence of his resurrection, how could they be faithful? The time Jesus spent in the tomb was the crucible of faith for his early followers. Until the coming of the Spirit at Pentecost, they hung suspended. Keating says that the disciples needed to let go of their former relationship with a Jesus they could see and hear and touch. They needed to grow into a new relationship with a Risen Jesus, whose sensible presence had been transformed and who remained with them in the Holy Spirit. Keating says, "Our crisis of faith will appear as a great invitation to go deeper into the heart of Christ…so that we may depend completely on the Holy Spirit. That is what spiritual maturity is."[20]

Keating identifies living in an abiding awareness of God's presence with having a mature faith, a faith that has been tried by fire. Eugene Peterson survived his own period of trial. After being disappointed in one congregation after another, and blaming God for giving him lousy congregations, Peterson came to a striking realization. He says, "Gradually it dawned on me that the crevasse was not *before* me, but *within* me."[21] The crevasse Peterson found within himself was his radical openness to God, not the God of success and notoriety, but the God of constant, abiding presence. As he gave himself more and more fully to God's mysterious presence, patience grew, humility surfaced, and love for his congregation returned. Now looking back at that time, Peterson says that it was life changing for him. Discovering the crevasse within, and the presence of God *within* the crevasse, rewrote the story of his second half of life.

The God who is within can withstand the most skeptical, the most belligerent sort of prayers. If our belligerence comes from a felt need for God, a rather desperate need, then we are more immediately in touch with God than we realize. Dorgan says, "Prayer does not mean the absence of questions, but rather probing them in the obscurity of faith, sinking into the abyss of mystery where we feel there is no foothold to steady ourselves."[22] Having no foothold throws even the most confident of us into doubt. But being in doubt about God and God's workings in our lives is a far cry from denying God. In fact, doubt and skepticism are necessary precursors to spiritual maturity. God, who understands completely, provides them for us as means to maturity. Keating says, "God has great sympathy for those who are going through this crisis in their spiritual lives. They do not know what is happening to them, and tend to concentrate on the disintegration of what they love, rather than on the real spiritual growth of which they are capable."[23] Shifting their concentration from what is being lost to what may be gained requires real faith.

Spiritual growth comes from God, not from us. In order to grow spiritually, we need to let go of the reins of our lives. When we make it, a sincere act of faith feels like a shot in the dark. If we knew what we were doing, it would not be faith. Eugene Peterson had to let go of his ambition of being the ideal pastor to the perfect congregation. Tom had to let go of his desire to ease his mother's suffering and to avoid her approaching death. The very difficult circumstances in which they found themselves brought each of these men to a critical moment, a moment of truth in which they had to decide where to place their trust. They both decided to walk in faith and discovered that "the crisis of faith is a confrontation with…God in our inmost being…It is to be brought inwardly face-to-face with the living God, who, faith assures us, dwells within us, and who, hope assures us, will reward those who seek him."[24]

Certainly, not everyone who travels through midlife experiences all three of the crises I have described: the crisis of limits, the crisis of meaning, and the crisis of faith. However, even one of these painful crises can be enough to disrupt the stability of our lives. At best, we resolve our crises by turning to God, who is present within us and within the crisis itself. At midlife we are perfectly positioned to make this turn. At midlife, as many writers tell us, the spiritual Self is burgeoning and will, if we cooperate, emerge.

Emergence of the Self

I am writing about the emergence of the Self in Northeastern Ohio in late winter/early spring. This year has produced near-record levels of snow and ardent desires for the change of seasons. But anyone who has ever lived in this part of the country knows that the quintessential sign of spring is the appearance of the crocuses—small, colorful, stubborn flowers that break through ice and snow and set the stage for the abundant springtime to follow. The remaining snowfalls of late March do not deter the crocuses. They are there, smiling, more numerous and more brightly colored than ever, when the sun melts the snow each day. In their courageous persistence, the crocuses remind me of the spirit within us, straining to break through the ambiguities of midlife.

It was Carl Jung who first hypothesized that an inner spiritual force, which he called the Self, initiates the tectonic shifts we associate with midlife. Jung claimed that we spend much of the first half of life conforming to the expectations of others—parents, teachers, employers, neighbors—and that conformity to external norms thwarts the development of our true, authentic selves. Nevertheless, he held that external forces could not daunt the movement of the Self within us. Like the crocus, the Self will emerge in its time. The more strenuously we try to quell it, the more vigorously it resists. The constant urging of the Self "represents a summons from within to move from the provisional life to true adulthood, from the false self to authenticity."[25] Of course, there are those who live authentically throughout their lives without problems. The majority of us would admit, however, that developing true authenticity represents a conscious commitment on our part. That commitment often solidifies during midlife.

Henri Nouwen, whose story began this chapter, is a case in point. Nouwen drew countless people to him through his preaching, teaching, and writing. Biographer Michael Ford reports that at the peak of his popularity Nouwen had to refuse fifty speaking engagements a week. When an assistant tried to help the notoriously disorganized Nouwen weed out his Rolodex, Nouwen could not part with a single entry. The frustrated assistant concluded that Nouwen had, at that time, sixteen hundred best friends! Because of his determination to maintain relationships worldwide, there were times when his phone bill was higher than his rent. Yet with all of his popularity, Nouwen suffered from an acute and unrelieved loneliness.

Ford detected the fault lines beneath Nouwen's dynamic confidence. He says, "He was an incredible teacher. I sensed just how much the students loved him. But there was something going on which meant he could not stay [at Harvard]. It might have been a growing loneliness. Or it might have been the discrepancy between who he was in an interior, personal sense, and the acclaim he was receiving from the students. My feeling was that somewhere there was a discrepancy between those two elements which became almost unbearable for him."[26] The discrepancy between the private and public aspects of Nouwen's life typifies the contradictions many midlifers endure. Ideally, midlife growth reduces or even eliminates the difference.

James Hollis characterizes the discrepancy between the external and internal aspects of life as a split between the external acquired personality and the internal Self breaking through. In the process of breaking through, the Self may unearth long-ignored experiences, especially those that were painful and unresolved at the time. Because the Self presses on to wholeness, it must open and address anything previously excluded from the personality. Hollis refers to the unresolved aspects of life as our inner dragons. He says, "Our dragons represent all that we fear and which threatens to swallow us; but they are also neglected parts of ourselves which may prove immensely valuable. In being taken seriously, even loved by us, they will respond by providing enormous energy and meaning for the journey of the second half of life."[27]

With compassionate help, Nouwen eventually realized that his desperate search for external affirmation hid a deeply buried need to be loved. He particularly grieved the loss of his mother's love, whose tender sensitivity was overshadowed in his early life by his autocratic father. Nouwen's insatiable need for love, and the mistakes in relationships that flowed from it, loomed as metaphorical dragons blocking his growth to true personal and spiritual adulthood. To his credit, Nouwen accepted the task of dealing with these issues, largely using spiritual tools. Always a deeply devotional man, he sought extended time for solitude and contemplation. Caring friends provided their homes as safe places where Nouwen could sort things out and prepare for a freer, fuller life. Among the outcomes of his painfully honest reflections was the decision to leave academia and move to a more hidden life of humble service at the L'Arche community at Daybreak.

Although very public, Nouwen's experience is not unique. Dragons of every description haunt the shadows of midlife. Loneliness, failure, abandonment, betrayal, loss—these and other dragon-types position themselves at the gateway to a peaceful, integrated later life. To our surprise, we have within us the power to slay them: the spiritual power of the Self. Midlife psychologist Kathleen Brehony says, "At midlife the power of the emerging Self is an awesome force that we reckon with, a confrontation nothing less than an encounter with the

Absolute. At midlife we question our relationship to God and the sacred and ponder the meaning of our existence."[28] It is far better to question and ponder than to ignore our relationship with God. Only by pondering and questioning can our relationship with God mature. Our emerging Self is naturally equipped for the challenge.

At this point the psychological vocabulary gives way to the religious. Psychology cannot reach God, the ultimate source of wholeness and healing, but the spirit within us can. Our spirit originated in God before we were born, and it will take us back to God at the end. Likewise, "the Self connects to our own 'ground of being'...to God, to all humanity, to all creation, through and beyond time and space."[29] If this is true, the ground of being to which the Self connects is the presence of God within us. If our innermost Self is connected to God, we have nothing to fear, threatening midlife dragons notwithstanding. God is love, and love casts out fear. Case closed.

The struggles of midlife cause us to speak in metaphysical terms, but we are still physical beings. Practically speaking, Nouwen had to adjust to a whole new life at Daybreak. Similarly, you and I must pay bills, go to work, care for our families. The difference is that we can now do so with transformed consciousness. The spirit, aware of God's presence within us, in touch with the divine presence, corresponds more easily with the presence of God in every person, event, and situation that we encounter, including the retreating dragons of the first half of life. In touch with God, we are free to relinquish any falsity with which we propped up the acquired, external self. We can live simply, forgive injuries, tolerate disappointments, and let go of useless anxieties.

Letting the spirit lead implies letting God lead, because we now realize that the two are intimately and inseparably connected. The spirit may lead us to unfamiliar territory, but we grow in trust as we proceed. Hollis says, "Even if I feel no floor beneath me, I still must take step after step, laying down a strip of accomplishment each time until I have built my own floor."[30]

The difference is that we do not build the floor alone. The midlife crisis clears the way for the emergence of the spirit, which is united with God. We will never be alone again. We never were.

Spirit Desires Meaning

Trappist monk Matthew Kelty was about sixty years old when he wrote his touching autobiographical narrative, *Flute Solo*. By that time he could reflect on a number of life changes, each of which brought him closer to what he felt at the time was his true vocation. All his life Kelty had struggled with opposite pulls in his personality: a strong desire for solitude, countered by an equally strong need for community. His partial attempts to find his way resemble the strokes of a pendulum, moving from extreme involvement with others in community to total solitude as a hermit monk. For a while after he made each move, Kelty was confident that he was doing God's will, that the transition had been worth the effort, and that his inner restlessness would finally be resolved. Each time the desire for a deeper meaning in his life moved him further.

Kelty's chronology included going through rigorous, intensely communal seminary training. The brotherly bonds of the seminary and the tightly controlled communal schedule intensified his desire for solitude. At long last, when the seminary training was complete, his missionary society sent him to the wilds of Papua New Guinea. There his ministry left him alone at the base mission for weeks at a time, while his coworker went into the highlands, and then reversed the process, when Kelty left his coworker alone and went into the highlands by himself. At first Kelty praised God for bringing him to an untouched place where he could finally enjoy some solitude. For a time, he thought he had it all; but soon the need for company began to plague him. He tells us, "I had not reckoned with loneliness. Sometimes when evening was coming on I could feel a great dark cloud settling on my soul like an oppressive weight." Instead of reveling in solitude, he was languishing in isolation. In the extremity of his loneliness, Kelty went straight to God and prayed, "You see how things are. You love me. If this is not going to work, get me out of here."[31]

Within ten days of that prayer Kelty was recalled by his society to edit their periodical magazine. He returned to the United States immediately and reentered the more familiar communal routine. For the eight years that Kelty edited the magazine, his thoughts returned often to Papua New Guinea. From his crowded editor's desk, the wilds of New Guinea shone with pristine beauty. Solitude beckoned as publishing costs increased, subscriptions decreased, and Kelty's heart sank. He knew he was not long for the publishing profession. Both he and the magazine were at their lowest point. Astonishingly, he tells us, "When the last issue was on the press, the plant caught fire at two o'clock one January morning and burned to the ground. I escaped from my quarters only by grace of a kindly Providence."[32]

Apparent failures at missionary work and at professional editing brought Kelty to a serious point. Without work, without an identifiable place in society, without any sense of direction, Kelty watched his world fall apart. He began drinking heavily and developed a cynical attitude. Following what appeared to be God's will had led him first to one ministry, then to another, without offering any satisfaction or affirmation at all. With the bare minimum of trust he had left, he once again sought help from God in prayer. He recalls, "I had the conviction that I was at a crossroads in my life and that some sort of resolution was called for."[33] He was right; we will return to Kelty's journey later in this chapter to discover with him what sort of resolution was in store.

Robert Stoudt's article, "The Midlife Crisis: God's Second Call," could have been written about Matthew Kelty's life. Stoudt outlines a kind of midlife crisis that he calls a "spiritual emergency." He says, "If ever there is a time in life when persons discover themselves to be in over their heads and helplessly, meaninglessly stuck, it is at midlife in this particular crisis experience."[34] Stoudt believes that spiritually inclined persons are particularly vulnerable to the crisis of meaning that lurks menacingly around midlife, since it undermines the worth of all of their previous commitments. Frequently these are persons who have sacrificed willingly, given generously, and offered leadership within their worshiping communities. Stoudt has known such persons to descend to a new low in life, feeling empty, without pleasure, drying up and withering away. At worst, he says, "The person in crisis begins quietly, desperately, to believe, if not hope, that death cannot be far away."[35] He is not speaking in hyperbole. The faithful person who has given all cannot believe that there is anything else left. It was at such a low point that Kelty cast himself desperately toward God, begging for mercy.

The striking incongruities of their lives throw Kelty and others into states of spiritual emergency at midlife. Many have raised their children, grown their businesses, served their churches. They have even cultivated lives of personal prayer. What could they possibly have done wrong? Indeed, they have not done anything wrong. In fact, they have done everything right. Yet nothing that they treasured in the first half of life now satisfies. Surely something else, something more will save them! But *what*? And *who*? They discover within themselves a "passion for ultimacy…a desire for some share in ultimate truth so as to have a basis for some ultimate commitment."[36] The desire for a deeper, more ultimate commitment spurs them further. In Kelty's case, seeking ordination to the priesthood was not enough, nor was accepting the missionary call to the wilds of New Guinea, nor was attempting to save a declining community publication. Apparent failure relentlessly beat back his hopes and challenged his faith.

Kelty's story parallels many midlife scenarios. Mark Gerzon says, "One of the signal events of…the middle passage is the recognition that, having achieved one's goals, one still hungers for more."[37] What differentiates the passionate, almost desperate hunger of midlife from the striving, grasping drives of the first half of life is that this later impulse comes directly from the spirit. The spirit urges us to make sense of our previous lives and to surpass them, not in terms of accomplishment, achievement, or success, but in terms of meaning and faith. Resolving a spiritual emergency demands a whole new repertoire of skills. "Concrete change is not the goal of the midlife passage. It is instead a time for introspection, reflection, integration and imagination."[38]

Desperation brought Kelty to his knees, and it kept him there until he could respond to his spirit's desire for still deeper meaning. Some time for thoughtful reflection stimulated his imagination to envision a life that might help him to integrate the conflicting pulls of solitude and community that had plagued him. Instead of demanding muscular effort, the spirit within him offered healing and wholeness. Looking back, Kelty writes, "I had spent half of a lifetime doing what they told me to do, pouring myself out in a frenzied effort to produce, to deliver, to come up with results." Much later he speaks even more vehemently, "Take your good works and be gone with them. I'll take my flute, the stars at night, my few books, the psalms. I'll manage somehow."[39]

A spiritual emergency at midlife propelled Kelty into the Trappist monastery of Our Lady of Gethsemane, near Louisville, Kentucky. There, through the grace of God, he met his real spiritual mentor, Thomas Merton, who helped him to gather up the shards of his earlier lives and to sculpt them into a grace-filled contemplative vocation. Kelty's vocation evolved into years spent in the community at Gethsemane, followed by a solitary period as a hermit back in Papua New Guinea and a later return to community. Now, at approximately ninety years of age, he speaks words of hope, trust, and inspiration to retreatants who come to the monastery with intense spiritual hunger as he did, so many years ago.

Encounter with the Absolute

We have moved fairly deeply into the midlife crisis. We have considered the possibility of undergoing a crisis of limits or meaning or faith. We have acknowledged the emergence of the spirit or Self within, and the spirit's insatiable desire for meaning. However, none of this brings relief to us as midlife travelers. In midlife, recognizing the limitations of many things we thought to be absolute forces us to ponder our own finitude. If we live long enough, we witness the fact that businesses, neighborhoods, institutions, and whole governments can rise and fall. Confronted with this reality, we cannot deny that our lives, too, will someday end. The shock of recognizing the shortness of life renders every moment of it more precious. Every moment, every experience, every decision matters. Far from being a death knell, the realization of our finitude invites us to live life more deeply. A glimpse of our own nothingness reveals the Absolute being that surrounds us. It brings us face-to-face with God.

Until God appears, however, we wander. Like Israelites in the desert worn out by the journey, we cry out to God. Surely there is some destination in sight. Surely we must be drawing near. Perhaps God will take pity on us and reach toward us from the other side. And just as God took pity on the Israelites, God also offers compassion to us. If we remain faithful in our darkest moments and through our lowest points, we may realize suddenly that God is with us, or more accurately, that we are with God. Of course this does not happen in all cases, but the reports of the experiences of many people suggest that an encounter with God is not beyond hope for any of us.

William James captured an impressive collection of first-person accounts of encounters with God in his landmark book, *The Varieties of Religious Experience*. One report was written by a struggling clergyman who went out to a quiet place above the city one evening to gather his thoughts. He says, "I remember the night, and almost the very spot on the hilltop, where my soul opened out, as it were, to the Infinite, and there was a rushing together of the two worlds, the inner and the outer. It was deep calling unto deep—the deep that my own struggle had opened up within being answered by the unfathomable deep without, reaching beyond the stars."[40] Perhaps this poor, embattled clergyman had reached the end of his rope. His soulful struggle had opened up inner space within him. His testimony suggests that, at least in his case, God entered in bringing fullness.

The clergyman is like many of us whose midlife events have created an opening toward God. Whether or not we recognize or respond, God is with us through every destabilizing event. At what appears to be the most inopportune moment, the divine presence may make itself known. As a matter of fact, some people remark that awareness of God begins as an uncomfortable feeling that they are being watched, or that someone they do not know is in the room with them. "Usually in the most surprising ways and at the most unexpected times, we are poignantly reminded that our privacy is being shared by an unseen and often uninvited Guest."[41] Thrown off by crisis, entertaining doubts, unsure of ourselves and of our future, we are in no mood for company.

The psychological dishevelment of midlife demolishes our defenses. Our proud, powerful self-image evaporates; feelings of omnipotence flee. We feel we are hanging by a thread. Amazingly, this is all for the spiritual good. "Spiritually speaking, the purposeful debilitation of the middle years is to undermine our smug sense of establishment and completion…The whole point of the inner fracas of the middle years is to demonstrate the fundamental spiritual fact that, regardless of how accomplished we are, we are not in control."[42] Surrendering control may be the antecedent of freely exposing our midlife mess to God, but in this condition, who wants a witness?

The reality is that God is already there, witnessing everything. The clergyman says, "The darkness held a presence that was all the more felt because it was not seen. I could not any more have doubted that *God* was there than that *I* was. Indeed, I felt myself to be, if possible, the less real of the two."[43] For him, there was no escape. He could not hide his midlife fears from God any more than we can. God is with us even if we experience only doubts and uncertainties. The fact that we are as we are, and that God is as God is, represents an absolute truth. The bond that holds these two realities together is love, God's unconditional love for us just as we are. There is no way, nor is there any need to prevaricate. God, who knows our innermost thoughts and loves our innermost being, abides with us.

Realizing that God abides with us changes us profoundly. We are immeasurably more free than we were in the first half of life. Our vision of reality more closely matches reality as it is. We have little or nothing to prove. Tolerance and acceptance grow. We extend to others the compassion we have received. We may be deeply humbled, but we are now indomitable. The spirit within us has encountered the God beyond us and discovered that we are inseparable. Regardless of circumstances or outcomes, we know that we are loved and cared for, and that *nothing* can separate us from the love of God. Having that awareness is having everything.

The midlife clergyman experienced this vividly. His encounter with God changed him completely. He reports, "Then if ever, I believe, I stood face-to-face with God and was born anew in his spirit. Since that time [nothing] has been able to shake my faith. Having once felt the presence of God's spirit, I have never lost it again for long."[44] The clergyman's epiphany captures the transcendent potential of the midlife crisis. Crisis shows us our own limitations, but in so doing, it may also reveal to us the all-knowing, all-loving presence of God. We who are finite derive our very being from God who is infinite. How could the very one who brought us into being ever fail us?

Having established this potentially reassuring resolution to the multiple crises of midlife, we will begin to consider some of the less reassuring states that may accompany them. Authorities from both psychological and spiritual perspectives will help us to distinguish among the states of depression, desolation, and spiritual dark night. Faithful people who pass through life's crises may experience one or more of these states, and understanding them better may provide encouragement. Readers of this book may have had firsthand experience with at least one of these states, and may benefit from learning more about them also. Pastoral counselors, spiritual directors, and religious psychologists will appreciate the distinctions made by these authorities as sensitive instruments for their work with those who are exploring the mysteries of midlife.

3
Accompanying States

Personal crisis spawns inner turmoil. Midlife crisis in particular generates an array of changes in the way people feel, think, and pray. In fact, it is not uncommon for faithful people who are immersed in midlife crises to doubt their ability to pray at all. Midlife crisis disrupts their previously consistent and comforting spiritual life and short-circuits their most sincere attempts to pray. For faithful people, the apparent loss of the ability to pray worsens the impact of the midlife crisis. Of all the losses they suffer, the loss of a felt relationship with God disturbs them most deeply. Emotional and spiritual repercussions may follow upon the perception of this most distressing loss.

Authorities from the fields of psychology and spirituality shed crucial light on the nature of some of the inner states accompanying midlife crisis. Psychologists outline the signs of depression, a common side effect of facing the impenetrable morass of midlife. Writers in the Ignatian tradition offer descriptions of spiritual desolation, an emotional response to the threatening temptations that complicate the crisis. Carmelite writers articulate the faith dimensions of the spiritual dark night, showing possible parallels to the midlife crisis' psychological traits.

This chapter will draw on all three sources of wisdom in order to enable midlifers and those who care for them to make some sense of the otherwise mystifying emotional and spiritual states that can occur in midlife. It will also attempt to show that, for faithful people, prayer during the midlife crisis may take on a more contemplative form than their previous ways of prayer. It will suggest that the unseen, unfelt presence of God during a crisis resembles the unseen, unfelt presence of God in contemplation.

Depression

Of the three states that this chapter will examine and compare—depression, desolation, and dark night—depression is by far the broadest category. Strictly speaking, depression is a psychological phenomenon, although it may occur simultaneously with spiritual desolation or spiritual dark-night experiences. Most adults and an alarming percentage of younger people have an unwelcome acquaintance with this enervating condition. For many, depression occurs rarely and is easily dismissed. For others, however, depression hangs like a pall over the emotional life. For anyone, midlife impasses may trigger episodes of depression that weaken their ability to cope with its challenges. The inability to change the circumstances of their lives may frustrate and demoralize them.

In her sensitive article, "Depression and Spiritual Desolation," Brigitte-Volaine Aufauvre depicts the plight of one midlifer who suffers from depression. At age forty, Edmund is considering being relieved of certain responsibilities that he has been avoiding for months. For Edmund, the thought of any activity seems like trying to move a mountain. He says, "All this struggle is exhausting me. I spend hours slumped in an armchair, unable to do anything; it would be better for me to be completely relieved of everything and go away for a rest."[1] Without detailing the sources of Edmund's suffering, we recognize in him the lethargy and despondency characteristic of depression. Earlier in his life he may have carried on dutifully. At age forty, he considers giving in.

Carmelite Kevin Culligan summarizes other familiar symptoms of depression in his comprehensive treatment of the spiritual dark night and psychological depression. First, he advises that anyone who suffers from several of these symptoms for a length of time should consult a physician and receive whatever therapy or medication may be recommended, regardless of what the symptoms may indicate spiritually. Then he lists several of the most frequently noted symptoms, including "a depressed mood…eating disturbances, sleep disturbances, low energy or fatigue, low self-esteem, poor concentration or difficulty making decisions, feelings of futility or hopelessness."[2] While a combination of these signs of depression would interfere with the smooth functioning of anyone's life, Culligan points out that people in midlife are exceptionally vulnerable to them. He says, "Menopause in women or retirement in men, while normal occurrences in adult life, may trigger…depression because they symbolize a loss of productive womanhood or manhood."[3] Loss, whether material or symbolic, sends tremors through the emotional life.

Loss surfaces as a recurrent theme in all of the literature dealing with midlife and its accompanying psychological and spiritual states. Midlifers have lost their youth, with all of its unlimited potential. Some have lost optimal health; others have lost employment or spouses. Many have watched cherished dreams disappear. Even those who seem from the outside to be personally connected and financially secure begin to realize interiorly that the end of life may be closer than the beginning. The end of life represents the greatest and most inescapable of losses. As such, it threatens most deeply. Of all of life's challenges, the realization of our own finitude and the finitude of all things may be the one that is most inevitable and the one for which we are least prepared. Midlife waves the banner of finitude in our faces. In doing so, it emerges as the most audacious adversary of our lives. No wonder midlife calls into question every inner resource upon which we have previously relied.

Returning to the hypothetical situation of Edmund focuses our attention on a specific type of loss that will be significant in later considerations: the loss of sense of self. In his earlier life, Edmund had envisioned himself as gifted and productive, and there was adequate factual basis for his positive sense of himself. He was intelligent, hardworking, goal oriented, and concerned about others. Achievements in early adulthood supported his justifiably favorable sense of self and amplified it. Because he was serious by nature and conscientious, relatives, friends, and employers piled responsibilities on him, responsibilities that he carried well. Praise and affirmation followed. At some imperceptible point Edmund began to think that he really *was* the extraordinary person others told him he was. He believed he really could carry unlimited levels of responsibility all by himself. At that point, his positive sense of self had evolved into an idealized sense of self, a self he could never become.

By midlife, unrelieved pressures and sustained responsibilities began to poke holes in Edmund's idealized sense of himself. The burden began to take its toll. As others continued to increase his responsibilities, Edmund began asking himself, "Who do they think I am?" The question conveyed his growing and understandable exasperation. But the more critical questions, the ones Edmund needed to ask himself, were different: "Who do *I* think I am? If I'm not *that* person, then who *am* I?" Asking these questions would have life-changing consequences for him. When Edmund grasps the reality of his situation, his initial reaction might be guilt for disappointing others, followed by anger at their manipulation of him and then blame of himself for being angry. If he moves through these negative reactions repeatedly, he enters a self-defeating cycle that leads to depression.

Edmund's sequence of reactions resembles a pattern Culligan describes. He says that the depression people suffer at midlife is often related to the deterioration of their earlier expectations of themselves. "Persons often feel deeply their loss of normal functioning, sometimes with anger turned in on themselves for their weakness of character, which then reinforces the feelings of low self-esteem that usually accompany depression."[4] The key word in Culligan's description is *normal*. Edmund had come to see as normal an idealized image of himself that was unattainable. Admitting that the idealized image is unattainable is the first step toward freedom from its brutal control. However, the admission that the idealized image is unattainable may be slow in coming.

In his treatment of the dark night and depression, Denys Turner says that depression ushers in a dislocation of selfhood. Awakening to the impossibility of becoming the person we thought we could become yields profound disappointment. A woman's discovery that she will never bear children undermines her long-held image of herself as a potential mother. A man's retirement from a position in which he had heavily invested robs him of the image of himself as a dedicated worker. Edmund's sudden urge to rid himself of all responsibility destroys his image of himself as reliable to a superhuman degree. Turner says, "Depression is a question all too clearly raised about what we *could* be like, accompanied by the despair of ever achieving it."[5] Yet despair is not the only option.

James Hollis suggests a healing element in the disappointment in oneself that hides at the heart of the midlife crisis. Hollis characterizes the abandonment of our idealized images of ourselves as a healthy withdrawal of projections. Insofar as our projections are unattainable, they need to be withdrawn. Insofar as Edmund thinks he is invincible, he is wrong. Earlier in life our projections may have motivated us; by midlife they taunt and shame us. Hollis says, "The limitations of our lives are suddenly inescapable…the bitterness and depression of midlife are linked to the amount of energy invested in…phantasmal wishes."[6] If we have invested a great deal of energy into phantasmal projections of ourselves, we will dispel them only with greater energy, but it will be energy of a different kind. Projections this powerful can only be cast out by prayer.

In early adulthood we construct unrealistic images of ourselves and use our willpower to try to live them out. Midlife deconstructs our idealized images by demonstrating the absolute limits of our willpower. Midlife shows us in no uncertain terms what we cannot do. Colliding with immovables and irreversibles in life reveals us to be the weak and limited human beings that we are. Edmund wonders, "If I'm not invincible, then what *am* I?" Still, wrenching as the dislocation of our idealized sense of self may be, it also holds the key to our liberation. Recognizing the phantasmal quality of our idealized self simultaneously releases its hold on us. Without the pressure of the idealized self, we are able to see ourselves as we really are, not as we imagine ourselves to be. What a relief.

Becoming more realistic about ourselves moves us into real adulthood, real maturity. However, the move comes at a cost. If we cling stubbornly to our idealized images of ourselves, the exposure of our inability to act will reverberate in our emotions as depression. If, on the other hand, we relinquish our idealized images, we open ourselves to a greater possibility: the possibility of becoming who we really are, rather than trying to be someone we cannot possibly be. Renouncing idealized images and letting go of hidden notions of our own omnipotence or perfection turns us toward the only ultimate source of these two powers. It turns us directly toward God. It allows God to be God in our lives. Rather than thinking everything depends on us, we learn to depend on God. This sounds like a viable solution, but in the midst of crisis we wonder how we can depend on a God who seems to have abandoned us.

Edmund is a religious man; his faith has sustained him thus far. But the intransigence of midlife shakes his faith. While earlier all things seemed possible, now too many parameters seem non-negotiable. Cornered by life, Edmund wonders, "Have I still got any faith? I am at the bottom of a quagmire, and it's no good for me to pray. God doesn't grant my prayers. Because of that I have gotten to the point of not being able to trust God anymore."[7] Perhaps God does not grant Edmund's prayers because they revolve around a false sense of himself. If that is true, the psychological phenomenon of depression may have spiritual ramifications for him. His depression may bring Edmund to a moment of free choice. Having exhausted his own resources, he may choose to surrender himself and his life to God. If Edmund can admit his own powerlessness and bitterness, if he can surrender to God as all-powerful and all-loving, everything changes. At that point it no longer matters that Edmund cannot attain his unrealistic goals. Nor does it matter that he cannot become his idealized self. Surrendering to God rearranges all of his priorities.

Surrendering to God, exchanging our priorities for God's priorities, our will for God's will—these are acts of spiritual maturity. Pastoral counselor John Coe says, "The spiritually mature have seen God work his will in their lives: he has taken their spouses, friends, and children; he has worked in a way that seemed confusing. In any case [they] have come to recognize through time that God is God of their lives, that God's will, not their own, is the central reality. He can do as he pleases, and is in fact invited to do so."[8] Edmund may not yet be at the point where he can invite God to do as he pleases in his life, but he is very near it. If God reaching out to Edmund can penetrate the depression surrounding him and touch the spirit within him, there is hope.

Earlier I noted that strictly speaking depression is a psychological phenomenon. Depression arises out of the way we think and feel, and it affects our ability to act. It is concerned primarily with ourselves, our relationships, or our surrounding circumstances. Nevertheless, because we are whole beings, the psychological is never far from the spiritual. Both are mutually implicated at all times, whether we realize it or not. Having considered the primarily psychological state of depression, we will now proceed to an investigation of two related states: spiritual desolation as it is described in Ignatian spirituality and spiritual dark night as it is described in the Carmelite spirituality of St. John of the Cross. Along the way we will search within the midlife crisis for connections between these states and the experience of contemplation.

Desolation

Back in the sixteenth century, as Ignatius of Loyola lay on his sickbed recuperating from the injuries of war, the earliest seeds of his spiritual system germinated within him. Bored and restless, as any vigorous warrior would be when confined to inactivity for months at a time, he sought out books to read for distraction.

Instead of the seductive courtly romances he usually read, he found only religious and spiritual books, including a popular life of Christ and a collection of the lives of the saints. Reading these books, however reluctantly, filled Ignatius' idle mind with visions of a different form of heroism than he had previously pursued. Gradually, a desire developed within him to imitate Christ and the saints, a desire that motivated him as intensely as his former urge to be a courtly knight. At times, in his characteristic love for the extreme, Ignatius was moved to give himself totally to the service of God. But the even more tantalizing hope of winning a high position at court and the love of a beautiful lady quickly replaced the noble prospect of doing that.

Empty hours of convalescence provided Ignatius with ample opportunity to consider his options for the future. Jesuit writer Charles Healy says, "He dreamed of emulating the deeds of St. Francis of Assisi and St. Dominic, but these reflections alternated in his mind with his dreams of romantic and military conquests."[9] While grand imaginings such as these are typical of adolescents, they are less common of grown men like Ignatius. After sustaining a physical trauma that effectively demolished his adolescent dreams, Ignatius was forced by circumstances to weigh his remaining possibilities. Of interest in the context of this study is the fact that Ignatius' dilemma occurred at age thirty and that he died at age sixty-four, placing his conversion experience at roughly the midpoint of his life. His consideration of alternatives took the form of midlife musings about how to go on, now that the time for youthful dreams had drawn to a close. With nothing but time on his hands, and little of interest outside him, Ignatius' attention turned inward.

From this period of prayerful reflection emerged Ignatius' spiritual notions about the discernment of spirits, spiritual consolation, and desolation. Simply put, the discernment of spirits is an attempt to understand God's working in our lives. The attempt is guided by our recognition of interior movements that would draw us closer to or further away from God. Ignatius recognized both types of movements within himself. When he considered the indulgent life of pleasure and romance, he enjoyed that option for a while, but was left feeling distinctly dry and empty shortly afterward. When he considered the spiritual life of sacrifice and service, he burned with desire to pursue it. Thoughts of life in Christ brought him deep peace and a sense of interior comfort that stayed with him long after his considerations were over.

Attraction toward God and things of the spirit won out over the pleasures that indulgence could offer Ignatius. In a decisive act he committed himself to respond valiantly to God's call. He had set out from Loyola headed for Jerusalem, and stopped along the way at the Benedictine monastery of Montserrat. There he spent several days in prayer, examination of conscience, and confession. Finally and with powerful symbolism, he "left his sword and dagger with his confessor to be placed in the church on the altar of Our Lady. He spent the night in prayer before the altar, an act that was reminiscent of the knightly vigil of prayer before battle. No longer would it be military battle for Ignatius, but spiritual warfare in which he would engage himself totally and heroically."[10]

The spiritual warfare that had waged inside Ignatius reflected the archetypical battle between good and evil. Forces of good and evil had contested each other for control of his soul during his days of physical and spiritual pain. Ignatius was well aware of their power. From his own experience he jotted down notes about the contradictory spiritual influences he called consolation and desolation. Later, for the guidance of others, he formulated precise understandings of these interior movements that everyone can acknowledge. Becoming aware of such movements and attempting to discover their spiritual meaning developed into a whole formula for the discernment of spirits, with specific rules for how to recognize and deal with them. Over time the prayer, self-examination, and resolution involved in this process of ongoing conversion took on a regular shape and became known as *The Spiritual Exercises*.

In *The Spiritual Exercises*, Ignatius addresses consolation first, because he believes that God prefers to deal with souls primarily by means of this movement. In times of consolation, he says, we are on fire with love for God. We see our lives and everything surrounding us within the context of God. We deeply regret our past offenses; nevertheless, confidence in the love and mercy of God sustains us. Faith, hope, and love increase and serve as powerful supports for actively serving God and others. We are in deep peace. On the contrary, in times of desolation we experience spiritual turmoil. Faith, hope, and love decrease in us, and we have little desire to pray or to serve God. "We will notice that the thoughts of rebelliousness, despair, or selfishness which arise at the time of desolation are in absolute contrast with the thoughts of the praise and service of God which flow during the time of consolation."[11] Sensitivity to these internal movements alerts us to their potential influence on us.

The treatment of both movements, consolation and desolation, and the placement of them in stark contrast with each other give evidence of Ignatius' appreciation for balance. In the process of discernment of spirits he weighed each potential experience by proposing its direct opposite in his imagination and allowing the interior effects of each possibility in turn to become apparent. A predominance of consolation usually indicated movement toward God; a predominance of desolation usually indicated the opposite. For the purposes of this chapter we will focus attention on the difficult and troubling state of spiritual desolation. Later we will emphasize the welcome and blessed experience of consolation.

Now let us imagine a character named Florence who underwent a midlife conversion similar to that of Ignatius. Raised without any religious influence, Florence wandered through adolescence and young adulthood. In her late thirties a failed marriage forced Florence to reevaluate her life. Sympathetic friends from work offered her support and invited her to become involved in a women's prayer group they attended. The cordiality of the group and their simple prayer attracted her. Through their influence and the spiritual direction she sought with their help, Florence received the grace of conversion. She entered an

RCIA program in the local parish and was baptized. An influx of the Spirit filled every void within her and brought her peace.

The grace of conversion came to Florence at a time when she was emotionally fragile. Although real, the grace was untested. Weeks after her baptism the contours of her life looked the same to her as they did before: her husband was gone, she felt like a failure, she faced the rest of her life painfully alone. In these circumstances her spirit was susceptible to discouragement. Her subsequent experience demonstrates several aspects of spiritual desolation. Desolation often follows a period of deep consolation and creates a strong contrast to it. The sudden loss of the felt consolation associated with her conversion cloaked Florence in darkness of soul. It confused her and interfered with her abilities to think and to choose. Over a period of time, her spirit became listless, tepid, and as though separated from its Creator and Lord. She wondered why she had gone through the steps of conversion at all. Other friends who had questioned her decision reminded her that they had warned her against the change. Doubt and discouragement erased all remnants of the joyful peace that conversion had brought her.

How could things have reversed themselves so drastically? Ignatius advises, "In time of desolation it is chiefly the evil spirit who guides and counsels us."[12] How could an evil spirit follow so closely upon the heels of a graced conversion? Why would an evil spirit trouble Florence now? Part of the answer rests in the fact that desolation is a spiritual state, and as such it is liable to spiritual warfare. In spiritual warfare both the sources and the destinations of the movements are spiritual. In this case the source of desolation is "chiefly the evil spirit," and the destination of the movement is Florence's soul. The desolation aims directly at Florence's wounded heart, intending to draw her away from sincere devotion to God. Only an evil and destructive spirit operates in this way.

Because we are whole persons, we cannot entirely separate spiritual distress from emotional or psychological distress. Florence's desolation of spirit reverberated in her feelings and emotions. She felt disheartened, downcast, abandoned, and alone. David Lonsdale affirms the probability of desolation producing these emotional signs, saying, "When there is discord, lack of coherence, conflict or resistance between the movement of grace and the person's understanding, will, desires, affections or intentions, there is an experience of spiritual desolation."[13] Probing discordant feelings like these for their spiritual sources returns us to the spiritual realm.

Jules Toner, a revered Jesuit specialist in these matters, highlights inner conflict as a key factor in desolation. He picks out five aspects of desolation that interact with each other: the action of the Holy Spirit, human faith and desire for God, antispiritual tendencies within a person, the influence of an evil spirit, and consequent spiritual desolation.[14] The first two affirmative factors (the action of the Holy Spirit and human faith and desire for God) conflict with the next two negative factors (antispiritual tendencies within a person and the influence of the evil spirit). The resulting spiritual struggle registers in the person as desolation.

Spiritual desolation brandishes an arsenal of temptations, often customized to correspond with the weaknesses of the person involved. For example, recollections of the consolations now gone may tempt Florence to try to recreate the conversion experience through her own effort. When she cannot evoke its comforting emotional impact, she may be tempted to doubt its authenticity. If the period of desolation continues, she may throw aside all spiritual practices as being worthless. She may succumb to temptation and abandon prayer. She may lose all interest in spiritual things, and become more cynical toward them in the future. If movements such as these occur, they will threaten the fundamental supports of her spirit. "The essential note of spiritual desolation is that it tends to undermine and destroy faith, hope, and charity."[15] Without these stabilizing and sustaining virtues, our spirits sink.

Florence now enters a spiritual crucible often found in a midlife crisis: the choice between despair and hope. Because desolation leads her to doubt God's care for her, she feels she has no supports left. Seeking baptism was a midlife risk for her, one that represented moving from despair over her own limitations to God, the unlimited source of hope. Now in desolation she begins to feel she has made a mistake. The God in whom she placed her trust seems not to care. In her spirit she must search deeply for the will to hope, and she must do so while feeling spiritually weak. Though painful, Florence's experience is not uncommon. In fact, "in Ignatius' descriptions of spiritual desolation the antispiritual with overtones of separation from God and increasing discouragement seem to predominate."[16] Negative overtones may predominate, but they need not prevail. The Spirit of God at work within the human spirit sustains hope.

Ignatius suggests four spiritual strategies for those dealing with desolation. First, we should try not to reverse a previous good choice, which is exactly what the evil spirit wants us to do. Second, we should try to fight off the desolation, perhaps by intensifying our prayer, taking on some penance, or examining ourselves and our life of faith. Third, we are to remember previous experiences of God's love and deepen our faith that God is with us now. Fourth, we are to persevere in patience, for in time the desolation will pass.[17]

Of the four strategies, the one that most energetically mobilizes our dormant spiritual resources is the second: fight off the desolation. At precisely the time when we feel most weak, the Spirit of God calls us to be most strong. This bold admonition is known in the Ignatian literature as *agere contra*, meaning the move "to fight against" the evil spirit at work in the desolation.[18] In this case, *agere contra* inspires the deliberate choice to fight against the forces of evil warring in our souls. If evil tempts us with thoughts of despair, we are all the more adamantly to choose hope. If the second half of life looks bleak, we are to plunge into it with ever-greater fervor. We are to rely on God for the power to do these things. When we choose to act this way, the very Spirit of God sustains us.

It is too soon to tell the story of Florence's next steps. We can imagine that she, like many other people undergoing trials, will choose to hope. Understanding the spiritual nature of the movements involved in spiritual struggles is a tremendous help to enduring them. We benefit from Ignatius' invaluable insights into the struggle, which are rooted in his own experience of the love and mercy of God. We need to be aware that the forces operating in spiritual warfare are beyond the realm of psychology. Fortunately, the spiritual resources required to deal with them are ready within us.

Dark Night

In 1577 in Toledo, Spain, leaders of an antagonistic faction of the Carmelite order arrested friar John of the Cross and threw him into a bleak prison cell. The cell measured roughly six by ten feet and had previously served as a closet or latrine. It had no window. The only light came from an opening a few inches wide high in the wall near the ceiling. John spent nine months in the dark cell deprived of his books, adequate food, decent clothing, and protection from the extremes of heat and cold. Three nights a week wardens took him to the refectory where members of the community took turns striking him with a rope, inflicting wounds that would not heal. They were punishing him for supposed disobedience and rebellion against their faction of the order, and for his association with Teresa of Avila and the Reform movement.[19]

Miraculously, it was while huddled in that prison cell that John composed in his mind exquisite spiritual poetry, most of which could not be put on paper until after his heroic escape. During the year following his imprisonment he wrote the poem entitled *The Dark Night* and developed the treatise explaining its meaning. Later, in *The Ascent of Mount Carmel*, John presented his whole spiritual system and the place of the dark night within it. The gloomy prison cell in Toledo gave birth to both works, and to the others that followed. Pertinent to the midlife emphasis of this study is the fact that "all his works that have come down to us were written during the last fourteen years of his life, between the age of thirty-six and forty-nine, after he had attained intellectual and spiritual maturity."[20] The journey to spiritual maturity taken by John himself and then shared with others serves as the context for the notion of the spiritual dark night.

In John's complex theory of spiritual development, the concept of the dark night plays a significant part. In fact, John's system envisions four different nights: active and passive nights of the senses, followed by active and passive nights of the spirit. The nights of the senses come earlier in the spiritual life and are more common, while those of the spirit come later and are more rare. All of the nights symbolize purification, detachment from everything but God, and growth toward greater and more complete union with God.

The first dark nights purify the senses. During the active night of the senses we discipline our desires and focus them more deliberately on God. Meanwhile, in the passive night of the senses, God draws us subtly toward deeper union. Gradually we lose interest in physical and emotional gratification and search more fervently for the spiritual fulfillment found only in God. At that point on the spiritual journey, "One's prayer life ordinarily becomes more contemplative. Persons now attend lovingly to God present in the depths of their own being and quietly open their interior self to receive the inflow of God."[21] After an indefinite period of time, perhaps years, God leads some people to the next phase in the spiritual journey, the dark night of spirit.

As the initial nights purify the senses, the further nights purify the spirit with its two noble faculties: intellect and will. In the active night of the spirit, we willingly detach ourselves from certain thoughts, ideas, and images to which we were previously attached. These active efforts of detachment serve to empty the intellect, especially of emotionally loaded images and memories, and most importantly of self-constructed notions of ourselves and God. At the same time we strive actively to redirect the will away from these intellectual constructs and more firmly toward

God. Approaching God by emptying the mind represents "the *via negativa*...which emphasizes that no images, ideologies, or cultural expressions can adequately convey all that God is, and revelation brings one into mystery."[22] While we voluntarily empty the mind and discipline the will in the active night of the spirit, God may enter in, beginning an even darker and more passive night.

Why do we undertake and endure such inner machinations? Ruth Burrows responds, "To answer this we must recall the fundamental truth that the heart must be totally purified of egotism if we are to receive God fully, 'annihilated' is not too strong a term...This is the essence of the night understood as purgation. It is the burning away of egotism, the death of the 'old man.'"[23] As we pursue the inner work of self-emptying, our own efforts gradually decrease in significance. Rarely, and independently of human effort, God takes over and becomes the guide through the passive night of spirit. Souls in the passive night of the spirit feel only desire and see only darkness. They walk in blind faith. God does the rest.

Although the correspondence is not exact, there are several ways in which John's experience parallels the experience of those in midlife crisis. As a youth, John so impressed his teachers that they selected him to study at a respected Jesuit school, and from there sent him to study at the prestigious University of Salamanca. As a young man at Salamanca, he so distinguished himself that he was appointed Prefect of Studies. A splendid academic career full of status symbols and material rewards awaited him. Peers acknowledged his intellectual gifts and his remarkable diligence. John had within his grasp all of the worldly goods that university advancement could offer. Yet, "the academic life did not attract him...He was drawn instead to contemplation in solitude before the Blessed Sacrament."[24] He could have collected enviable external signs of achievement, but his spirit craved something more.

When John met Teresa of Avila, the next step of his spiritual journey became clear. His love of voluntary poverty and physical austerity attracted him to the Teresian Reform movement. In the Reform he disciplined himself through external means: spending hours in prayer, observing days of fast, wearing threadbare clothes, sleeping on hard beds, and living in dilapidated buildings. Although severe, these penitential practices brought him inner freedom and spiritual joy. His ascetical life matched what he would later call the active night of the senses. Meanwhile God drew John passively and ever more deeply into contemplation. As God's influence increased, John's remaining attachments to all other things decreased. Through this process God led John to what he would later call a passive night of the senses.

We may infer that when his captors threw John into the dank cell in Toledo, they changed the prospects for his life drastically. By imprisoning him they took from him not only the minimal physical supports he had in the Reform community, but also his hopes for the spread of the Reform itself. John had long since given up comfort and pleasure, the gratifications of the senses. In their place, he had directed his fine mind and passionate heart toward the idealism and authenticity of the Reform, goods of the spirit. Early on he had responded to the call to contemplation and had enjoyed deep intimacy with God. In time he had come to associate his work in the Reform as a way of sharing that intimacy with others. We can imagine that suddenly, from his narrow prison cell, his hopes for himself and for the Reform seemed to be lost. Only the presence of God sustained him, and God may have seemed very far away.

The nights of the spirit are rare occurrences, so it may be presumptuous to try to associate them too closely with any human experience. However, if there is any human narrative that encompasses their dynamics, it is probably John's own. We may imagine that the confinement of his prison cell left John with long hours of solitude in which to ponder and to pray. If he turned his mind away from specific hopes for the Reform and his own role in it, if he directed his will continually toward God and God's will, he would be practicing the emptying of the mind and strengthening of the will that he later described as the active night of the spirit.

If God continued to draw nearer to John in mysterious, unseen, unfelt ways, without offering comforting fantasies of the success of the Reform or of John's own successful escape, then God would be leading John through the passive night of the spirit. The active and passive nights of the spirit would be bound together, uniting John's ardent desire and deep faith with God's constant, unfailing presence to him in darkness.

John's descriptions of the dark night are undoubtedly rooted in his own experience. For the benefit of others, he portrays darkness eloquently, poignantly. The dark night is full of desire and colored by pain. In it deep longing for God constantly confronts the apparent absence of God. Acute spiritual frustration generates a variety of emotional reactions: desolation, anguish, confusion, grief, unworthiness and other interior pain. However, lest we despair, pulled down by such emotional weight, John assures us that these symptoms of the dark night are merely "the effects of God's increasing self-communication."[25] In the passive night God enters the human soul by blindingly bright self-communication. Because the human cannot comprehend the divine, it perceives the approach of the divine only as mysterious darkness.

So, we need to distinguish the spiritual state of the dark night from the emotional reactions to it. Spiritually, God communicates directly with the soul; emotionally, the soul perceives only darkness. Spiritually, God is at work in the soul; emotionally, the soul feels powerless, disarmed, paralyzed. Why such paradoxical dynamics? Of what spiritual benefit can they possibly be? In response, Colin Thompson suggests specifically, "John of the Cross' 'solid and substantial doctrine' is provided for souls in crisis…These moments of crisis may be points of transition to the next stage of the journey, instead of insurmountable obstacles to its continuation."[26] The acute desire for God, paired with the apparent absence of God, prompts a spiritual crisis potentially leading to spiritual growth.

Midlife pilgrims often experience emptiness and dryness, and they fear the absence of God. Life's transitions throw them into confusion and disorientation. In their worst moments, they feel deaf, dumb, blind, and paralyzed. God, in whom they had placed their trust, seems to have abandoned them. God offers no explanations for midlife mysteries and little respite from their pain. Why? To what purpose? Why not, for example, just release John from his prison cell? Why not implement the Reform by divine intervention? Why must John suffer alone, in darkness, wishing only to be with God and to live for God? Similarly, we wonder whether our midlife misery is some sort of punishment. If so, for *what*?

Speaking for John, Michael O'Connor addresses these pressing questions. He suggests that periods of darkness move individuals out of spiritual complacency and into spiritual maturity. Just as detachment from the senses leads us to the spirit, so darkness in the spirit leads us more directly to God. In fact, he says, "John of the Cross considered darkness a normal, inevitable aspect of growth toward religious maturity."[27] For John, the essence of religious maturity is detachment from all that is not God followed by deeper, more profound faith in God. Only passive receptivity to God's action in the soul allows for such change.

Religious maturity requires dismantling all of our former images of God and of ourselves. In spiritual darkness we learn to love God as *God*, not just the gifts of God or our human conceptions of God. God enters in darkness precisely to expose the inadequacy of our former conceptions. Receiving God as God, and not as our conception of God, moves us from spiritual adolescence to spiritual maturity. In darkness, we survive only on faith, and our faith deepens as God's darkness works on us. "Grace perfects nature…The Spirit is doing the transformation upon and within the human soul. Thus, the work of the Spirit takes place within a natural, developmental psychological history already in process."[28]

Midlife itself takes place within a natural developmental history. We arrive at midlife having accomplished the important tasks of childhood, adolescence, and young adulthood; but we are not yet finished. Nor are we satisfied. Spiritually, the most difficult and the most fulfilling experiences await us. As the complexities of midlife throw us back on ourselves, we begin to comprehend our inability to solve them entirely on our own. We realize vividly our need for God, our total dependence on God. "By facing the darkness, individuals confront the void within where there was once spiritual sustenance…They begin to move beyond the confusion and encounter an opportunity for profound repatterning of lives that are centered on God. Rather than maladies to be fixed, the challenges that are encountered on the inward journey call for more being than doing."[29]

Both midlife crisis and spiritual maturity call for more being than doing. Both reveal the inadequacies of our active striving. Both introduce us to the uncertainty and radical openness of simply being. The invitation to shift our attention from ourselves and our own efforts to God and God's mysterious action terrifies most of us. It demands the renunciation of skills and strategies that previously undergirded our lives. Eventually, we must decide between terror and trust. Left to our own devices, we would continue to live in terror. Surrendering to God, we begin to live in trust. It may be the most important decision of our lives.

Similarities and Differences

Among the three states addressed in this chapter—depression, desolation, and dark night—similarities and differences abound. To examine these, we will begin by describing the characteristics that the three states have in common, and then go on to delineate differences among them. The most general of the three states is depression, which people experience primarily as an emotional or psychological condition. The other two states, desolation and dark night, are primarily spiritual in nature. Depression may occur independently, with no spiritual complications; or it may occur simultaneously with either desolation or dark night. The two states that do not appear together are desolation and dark night, for reasons that will be explained.

Similar emotional indicators describe all three states: a profound sense of loss, leading to sadness; a feeling of being abandoned or left alone, leading to lower self-esteem; feelings of failure, leading to generalized hopelessness; and anxiety about oneself and one's future, diminishing the positive prospects in sight. In other words, the person suffering from any of the three states we are considering inhabits an emotionally dreary landscape. In depression the emotions predominate and little or no attention is given to spiritual implications, unless spirituality is important to the depressed person. In both desolation and dark night, spiritual implications predominate and symptoms of depression may or may not be addressed, depending upon the needs of the person.

Psychological and spiritual authorities agree that if the person suffers from several of the recognized signs of depression mentioned earlier in this chapter, they should seek professional psychological help first, and deal with the spiritual implications of depression secondarily. In fact, Gerald May cautions, "If one is to err in this, it is probably better to label a true spiritual desolation as depression than the reverse."[30] Because grace builds on nature, care for depression coming from human nature takes precedence over care for the more delicate spiritual conditions of desolation and dark night. So, the first distinction we make concerns the nature of the person's distress. If it is primarily emotional, we deal with depression as a malady of the imperfect human condition. If it is primarily spiritual, we must distinguish further between the two remaining conditions, desolation and dark night.

Probably the most important difference among the three states is their source. Depression traces its source to either historical or biological roots, while the roots of both desolation and dark night are spiritual. Historical sources of depression include family disturbances and social or work-related events of the recent or distant past. Negative remnants of these experiences cast a shadow on the emotional life. Inability to resolve them either in the real world or in one's mind weighs down the psyche. Correlatively, biological sources of depression include chemical imbalances requiring medical treatment and the effects of physical trauma or chronic pain. In addition, Lonsdale mentions taking into account "factors such as fatigue, stress, burnout…bereavement, illness, and age"[31] as possible human-level influences leading to depression and having potential side effects on the spiritual life.

Clarifying the sources of desolation and dark night requires a further distinction. While the sources of both of these states are spiritual, they approach the person from essentially different spiritual directions. Ignatius locates the source of desolation in the evil spirit, who he says tempts and troubles the soul. In desolation the evil spirit aims at weaknesses in human nature, and attempts to use them to pull the spirit down. John of the Cross locates the source of the dark night in the Holy Spirit, who he says infuses the soul with divine light. In the dark night, the Holy Spirit aims at the presence of God within the human soul and moves to increase God's transforming action there.

Evil spirit versus Holy Spirit. More opposite sources for the inner movements described here could not be identified. Actually, it is on this point of opposition of the sources of desolation and dark night that Jules Toner says they are most radically different.[32] By reason of their extremely differing origins, it is impossible for desolation and dark night to appear together. Toner allows that the evil spirit may attempt to thwart the action of the Holy Spirit during the dark night, but he stipulates that in competition with the Holy Spirit, the evil spirit plays only a minor role.

A second point of contrast between desolation and dark night is their treatment of the phenomenon of desire. Ignatius warns that when faithful souls undergo desolation, the desire for God and the things of God wanes. It is replaced with Ignatius' famous "inclination to what is lowly," meaning an attraction to mere physical and emotional pleasures, as opposed to pure spiritual desire. In John's system, desire stimulates the spiritual disciplines of the active nights, and it becomes even more important in the passive nights. In fact, desire becomes most intense in passive darkness. Passive darkness arouses unsatisfied desire that all the more ardently searches for God.

A third discrepancy among the states is the focus of their attention. Depressed persons focus on themselves, their relationships, and their life situations, without necessarily referring to God. In contrast, persons in desolation and dark night focus on relationship with God, and on their personal relationships and life situations as they impact relationship with God. In depression the focus is more generalized and diffused: everything seems to be wrong, nothing seems to work, hope for improvement seems to be dim. In desolation and dark night, on the contrary, the focus is more refined and specific.[33] Some particular thing interferes with the person's ongoing relationship with God. In Ignatian desolation, it is the evil spirit. In John's darkness, it is the Spirit of God. Some significant quality of the spiritual life has changed. In desolation, it has changed for the worse, and in darkness, for the better. Faithful people want to know what interferes or what has changed, and why. In both cases, they want to clarify the situation and grow closer to God.

A fourth disparity among the states is the dimension of loss. Michael O'Connor notices, "Loss for the depressed client is usually secular in nature: loss of a dear one through death or the termination of a relationship, or loss of a job, finances, or health, any of which can precipitate a loss of life's meaning." O'Connor refers to these losses as "more secular in nature" than the spiritual losses experienced in desolation and dark night.[34] Often, as a practical consequence of the concrete external losses mentioned, the depressed person also loses the ability to function efficiently and to relate with others compatibly. Depression makes the person sluggish and irritable and inclines him to withdraw from others.

By contrast, the comparable states of desolation and dark night notice spiritual losses. In desolation, there is a loss of fervor. Individuals in desolation lose interest in prayer and become lukewarm in relationship to God. Desolation dampens desire in them and spiritual growth grinds to a halt. The dark night, on the other hand, creates a loss of the felt presence of God. Desire increases, because individuals fear they have lost their relationship with God. Increased desire prompts continuing spiritual growth. It is worth mentioning here that, if persons in either desolation or dark night are not simultaneously depressed, they will continue to function efficiently and relate satisfactorily with others. No one else may suspect that internal movements are at work. Only the struggling persons or those in whom they confide will know. For that reason competent psychological counseling and/or spiritual direction take on greater importance at these times.

The fifth point of comparison observes the effects of each state. This issue dramatically differentiates desolation from the dark night. The distinction revolves around the virtues of faith, hope, and love. Tradition calls these the theological virtues because their object is the very being of God in whom we place our faith, in whom we hope, and whom we most deeply love. The two spiritual states we are studying have opposite effects on these virtues. Spiritual desolation decreases them, whereas the dark night increases them. The striking difference in effects relates to the opposite sources of the two states. Because the evil spirit provokes desolation, evil action directly attacks the strong bonds of virtue that connect the soul with God. Because the Holy Spirit operates in the dark night, divine action directly affirms and strengthens them.

A final difference between desolation and dark night has to do with the advice offered to people in these states. Again, the contrast is striking. Ignatius exhorts faithful souls to work against the evil influence within the desolation. His *agere contra* admonition captures that attitude. In Ignatius' system, the person's activity plays a major role. The person in desolation must work diligently against temptations and the attacks of evil. By contrast, John's advice to souls in the dark night is that they become more passive. If they try to use willpower to dispel the darkness, they may find themselves fighting against God! "Failure to distinguish" between desolation and dark night, says

Toner, "will lead to struggling against the infused light of God as if it were the power of evil, instead of yielding and waiting while the light painfully but lovingly purifies and gives life."[35] Discernment between these two states guides the spiritual direction of those who experience them.

Among the three states, depression is the broadest and most easily addressed in today's psychologically astute climate. Because of its life-inhibiting repercussions, depressed persons do best to seek help from qualified psychological professionals, assuming good psychological care allows for subsequent attention to spiritual care. Authorities in both Ignatian and Carmelite circles agree that between the two spiritual states, desolation comes earlier in the spiritual life and is a more common problem. Dark night comes later and is less frequent. Still, both states call for sensitive handling by wise and holy spiritual directors. Any one of these troubling inner conditions or any combination of them together may emerge in the difficult time of midlife. The transitions that typify midlife may produce unfamiliar and unsettling psychological and spiritual dynamics. If they do, midlife pilgrims would do well to consult about any disturbing inner workings with experienced, knowledgeable people who can help.

This chapter has tackled the daunting task of discriminating among three elusive and mysterious inner states. These conditions may occur in midlife, even if they have not appeared before. Authorities cited in this chapter provide helpful criteria for diagnosing midlife conditions and for locating their psychological and spiritual sources and implications. Chapter 4 will continue the comparison between human and spiritual development, especially during midlife. Specifically, it will compare the emerging experiences of midlife with those of contemplation. For faithful people who encounter turbulence in their spiritual lives in the middle years, the similarities may offer affirmation and hope.

4
Experiential Signs

People who live on earthquake faults sense the tremors of an impending eruption and react instinctively. They grab their children and run outside to avoid flying glass and collapsing ceilings. When the quake has passed they assess the impact, scanning for immediate effects on themselves and on the environment. If there are no broken bones and only minor scratches, shattered windows and falling plaster, they consider themselves lucky. In time they search out family and friends, clear away debris, and begin the rebuilding process.

Similarly, personal crisis sends shock waves through the entire human system. It takes people by surprise and affects them in ways they only vaguely recognize. Something has changed without their knowing it. They wonder what has happened, or what is going to happen? They realize that, temporarily at least, they have lost control of the situation. Like people who live on earthquake faults, midlife searchers who sense the tremors begin checking to see whether everything is all right. They may have incurred physical, emotional, or spiritual damage. Things are not as steady and predictable as they were before. Hearing the stories of others who have survived comparable crises provides a framework within which they can find their bearings.

This chapter will consider some experiential signs of midlife crisis, including loss of identity, anxiety over the inability to control, and an awareness of inner emptiness. Midlifers who experience these signs may be encouraged to hear that they also appear in some descriptions of contemplation. Several contemporary spiritual writers have recorded their experiences of moving through crisis and of dealing with these issues using contemplative practices. Their stories include references to how their personal crises related to their prayer. Sue Monk Kidd and

Margaret Silf offer realistic examples of loss of identity. Thomas Merton describes human and spiritual anxiety or dread. Cardinal Bernardin and Margaret Guenther record the sobering and freeing effects of inner emptiness. Considering their experiences can provide guidance for others struggling with the same matters.

Loss of Identity

"I'm sitting alone reading the newspaper. I turn to the classified ads, hoping that I'll discover something new for my life. Suddenly I come upon an article that announces my death. I'm stunned. How did my obituary get in the want-ads, I wonder?"[1] This is how Sue Monk Kidd retells a dream that came to her during a period of midlife searching. At that time, like many women, Kidd was married and had children. Like some midlife women, she had achieved notable success. Her whimsical book, *The Secret Life of Bees*, had made the *New York Times* best-seller list. Impressive crowds attended her lectures. She acted as mentor and confidante to numerous young writers and career women. How could she be anything but happy?

At the time of her symbolic dream, the spinning wheels of Kidd's life were mired in discontent. She recalls, "I was standing on the shifting ground of midlife, having come upon that time in life when one is summoned to an inner transformation, to a crossing over from one identity to another." Many women would gladly have traded identities with Kidd. How dare she question or change anything? She had a loving husband, healthy children, a gracious home, and a better-than-average career path.

Despite a sharp awareness of the blessings in her life, Kidd sensed some missing quality. She describes her experience as a crisis of the spirit, a need to grow deeper, to cast off false layers of ego identity and become the true self God intended her to be. Even though she was already a person of faith, the invitation to spiritual transformation emerged in her life as an unwelcome upheaval. She lamented, "Each day I went about my responsi-

CONTEMPLATION AND MIDLIFE CRISIS

bilities as always, writing in the morning, picking my children up…answering mail, shopping for groceries, cooking…Outwardly I appeared just fine. Inside I was in turmoil." No wonder her dream featured fantasies of her death.

The mismatch between Kidd's inner and outer identities alerted her to a crisis of the spirit. She resolved to make no moves until she sensed some better direction from God. Only a prolonged period of sincere waiting brought her peace. For months she waited patiently upon God, in whom she slowly found her true self. She does not refer to her time of patient waiting as prayer, but it has all the earmarks of contemplation. She sat still, she became silent, she deflected the impulse to act. Finally, being at peace with God helped her to put all other aspects of her life into perspective. Without abandoning husband, children, or career, she returned to them as a different person. God's peace steadied her heart and flowed through her to the many others she loved and cared for.

Margaret Silf, another female author, went through a similar midlife identity change. As a young adult, she wrote computer programs for a respected company. She remembers nostalgically that the workplace was less pressured then. The company's offices were located in a natural setting that allowed for leisurely walks along a nearby canal during long lunch breaks. Although she liked her job and was good at it, she lost that position without warning. Looking back, she says, "All kinds of unpleasantness have intervened between those happy memories and the place where I find myself today, including the loss of that job and the relative security it held for me…Life hurts everyone in some way or other as the years go by."[2] Loss of employment at midlife shatters a worker's identity. Whether it comes through retirement, restructuring, or layoff, unemployment drastically shakes the sense of self. The shift generates far-reaching personal, financial, and spiritual aftershocks.

Silf eventually signed on with an agency that did short-term temporary work for other companies. Ironically, one of her assignments took her back to her original company for a week's work. She describes her first day there: "Here I was, just a contractor back in the place I had worked for so many years. I hardly knew anyone there now, and hardly anyone knew me. I was at a different desk each day, wherever there happened to be space, using a borrowed laptop computer plugged in wherever I could find a vacant socket." She had gone from being a valued employee to being a temporary nuisance. The sense of belonging she had taken for granted was painfully missing. Being seen as a mere "temp" dealt her ego a serious blow.

One day during the assignment, Silf went outside during her lunch break and took the familiar walk by the canal that she had enjoyed so often. The walk turned into a moment of grace, in which she could see how she had changed since leaving there. She says, "The walk, stolen out of the middle of a hectic day, became a prayer and gave me a perspective on my own life's journey that permanently changed my way of seeing things." Silf's deliberate step outside, and her willingness to accept the very different identity she brought to her old work situation, freed her in many ways. Because she opened herself to the experience, sun, trees, water, and breezes all reminded her of God's provident care. She stayed within the sense of God's providence as she returned to work. Awareness of God's love for her sustained her there, and helped her to see her lowered employment status as unimportant in comparison.

Loss of identity also appears as a factor in descriptions of contemplative prayer. Contemplation unites the person with God, so that the sense of a separate identity disappears. United with God, the person is neither spouse nor parent, neither author nor reader, neither worker nor unemployed. In God all things are one. Situating identity loss within the context of the passive night of the spirit, Denys Turner says, "The union of God and soul is such that they no longer exclude one another in either way. If I can have no identity as contrasted with God's, then my identity with God cannot be opposed to my identity with me."[3] In God, we are who we are. No further distinctions are necessary.

The turmoil of midlife can throw us into a period of darkness in which we do not recognize ourselves. We are no longer who we were, but we do not yet know who we will become. If we are faithful, accepting the darkness brings us into deeper union with God. Contemplatives teach us that remaining in darkness for a time allows us to find God present there. Secure in God's presence, the shifting, changing identities of midlife simply do not matter. When nothing else is clear to us, God somehow draws near. In new and unexpected ways, we relax into God's presence. Although our external circumstances do not change, our inner capacity for dealing with them mysteriously and permanently expands. Although we lose a familiar former identity, we find a deeper spiritual identity in God.

Irreconcilable Opposites

Midlife is full of contradictions, some of which are painful and some of which are amusing. Inner dialogues like Sue Monk Kidd's reveal underlying fault lines. "I had been maintaining a heavy speaking schedule, and the number of engagements was wearing on me. 'Why are you compelled to do so many?' I asked myself. 'Why not cut them in half?' Part of me wanted balance, wanted to cut back. The other part said, 'If you cut back, you'll diminish your career. Everyone knows you have to promote yourself if you want to get ahead.'"[4] Becoming aware of conflicting movements in herself and presenting the alternatives to God in prayer helped Kidd decide to reduce her professional schedule and live in deeper peace. Impulses to return to a hectic pace continued to trouble her, but when she brought them to God in stillness, she could put them in their proper place.

The resolution of Margaret Silf's period of crisis included becoming involved in Ignatian spirituality. Learning about Ignatius and practicing his methods of prayer and discernment opened a whole new world to her. Over time she participated in Ignatian prayer groups, received training, and became a compassionate spiritual director. One aspect of Ignatian spirituality that fascinated her was the idea of finding one's deepest desire. In

Silf's case, discovering prayer and the life of the spirit stirred desires in her that the world of work could never satisfy. With good humor she says, "In my day job, I am writing a programmer's guide on how to overcome the problems in computer data management...I sometimes think my PC will give a little shudder of culture shock when I expect it to process my thoughts on the problems of two-digit notation and search for my deepest desire at the same time."[5] Only God can create capacities of such striking contrasts in the same human being. Learning to live our contrasts gracefully is the task of a lifetime.

Jungian psychologists and spiritual directors agree that irreconcilable opposites emerge within us more forcefully at midlife than they do earlier. Their power derives partly from an innate human drive toward wholeness and integration. Neglected aspects of us demand attention and can no longer be denied. At midlife, serious people discover the temptation to play. Passive people notice suppressed anger. Computer programmers become spiritual directors. Admitting inner contradictions like these, and allowing the tensions they create to bring us to greater wholeness, promotes both human and spiritual development. Spiritual psychologist John Coe thinks that many believers at this point "struggle back and forth between feelings of failure and a minimal obedience, their hearts filled with warring passions. However, what they often miss...is that God actually intends to bring forth these warring, sinful passions (unhealthy hopes, desires, loves, and angers) from the depths of the heart."[6] God intends to bring them forth only to heal them and to make us whole, not to deepen the inner fissures that the first half of life has created.

Acknowledging our own contradictions exposes any layers of falsity we have developed. Because eradicating them totally is not within our power, we do best to learn to live with them nonviolently, having the same compassion for ourselves as God has for us. "Out of love we take up the tensions of our darkness voluntarily, for the sole purpose of emerging to a more genuine life in which God's image is enlivened within us."[7] Contemplatives highlight the spiritual potential in the act of confronting contradictions. Ignatius contrasts consolation and desolation. John of the Cross sees bright darkness and hears silent music. God, who is beyond all contradictions, mysteriously brings them into one. When we patiently present our contradictions to God in silent stillness, tensions disappear and healing wholeness comes.

Personal Weakness

One of the reasons identity shifts at midlife is that we find it more difficult to ignore personal weakness as we mature. Whether it manifests itself in poorer eyesight, slower reactions, or decreased energy, the onset of weakness in the middle years challenges earlier notions of invincibility. Because we know ourselves and the world better by midlife, all but the most stubborn among us must admit that we are flawed and that the world is imperfect. Especially if crisis has caused us to look within ourselves, we encounter both strength and weakness there. We realize that we have within us both darkness and light. We are both sinner and saved.

Contemplatives are familiar with paradoxical phenomena such as strength and weakness, sin and salvation. Their contemplative presence to God, who is beyond all comprehension, sensitizes them to the paradoxical in life. They learn that only God encompasses the ultimate resolution of opposites. Only God holds justice and mercy in perfect balance. Only God uses the weak to confound the strong. Carmelite writer Margaret Dorgan says that in sustained presence to God, it is not unusual for contemplatives to "recognize fresh strengths even while being more acutely aware of personal weakness." Awareness of personal weakness facilitates an ongoing process of conversion. In the process, "inner purification wrestles with human nature in order to heal it."[8]

Personal weakness cries out for healing. Even if our weaknesses have no moral implications, they provoke in us a vague sense of brokenness and guilt. Something seems to be wrong, but we cannot identify what it is. We seem to have failed, but we cannot specify how. Some of us have really sinned and carry within us an authentic need for repentance and forgiveness. Most of us, however, only feel the generalized consequences of the weakened human condition. Like all other humans, we suffer the effects of original sin. Dealing with its effects constitutes a recurring theme in the spiritual life. Thomas Keating believes, "Spiritual progress consists first of all in embracing the reality of original sin as it exists in ourselves, but without despairing."[9] Embracing sin? Is this just another perplexing contradiction? At worst, grappling with the reality of sin tempts us to despair. At best, recognizing God's overwhelming love for us, despite our sinful condition, moves us to thanks and praise.

Margaret Silf, the computer programmer turned spiritual director, employs a vivid metaphor for dealing with realized weakness. Silf had lived in Berlin years before, when the wall dominated the landscape. Watchtowers, guards, mines, and barbed wire separated East Berlin from West. The image of that fortification returned to her one day during prayer, as she became more conscious of her weaknesses. She confesses, "I was like the beleaguered city, and that was exactly how I felt when I started to realize my separateness from God…Like a besieged city, I was surrounded by unscalable walls and hostile guards; I was occupied by enemy forces…At first I could feel only the despair of the situation and my absolute helplessness in it."[10] Fortunately, she did not remain long in that desolate place.

Silf is a woman of faith who desired to grow in the life of the spirit. Gradually, perseverance in prayer turned her attention away from her own sinfulness and toward the love and mercy of God that infinitely overshadows it. Ironically, she could not truly appreciate God's love and mercy until she had first recognized her own weaknesses. Only when she grasped her separateness from God could she seek a deeper degree of union. Others come to the same turning point that Silf did as they endure midlife trials. Their musings bring to mind troubling memories of faults, weaknesses, or real sins. Humbling as their radical personal honesty may be, it gives them the opportunity to seek reconciliation and forgiveness from God. If they can open themselves to it, God's response of unconditional love sets the tone and direction for the rest of their lives.

Emotional Pain

We do not touch our personal weakness without feeling emotional pain. Nor do we jettison familiar ego identities without distress. For example, celebrated author Sue Monk Kidd suffered emotionally as she perceived how her time of transition affected her marriage. She says, "Like most crises, the midlife trial is a complexity of feelings…a vague sense of grieving and loss…With the breakdown of the false selves came the fear that the earth under my feet was melting away. Then what? I wondered. It was an empty feeling, an odd kind of mourning."[11] Even false identities create a vacuum when they leave. Until a new spiritual identity takes shape, we suffer from the loss of the old. Unsure of what will replace it, we feel vulnerable in the extreme.

Ian Matthew uses John of the Cross' language and imagery to capture this feeling of vulnerability. In describing John's dark night he says, "This is the night where there is not only pain, but where the ground I stand on to face the pain seems to shift…It may cut deep…It may strike at the level where I connect as a person."[12] It is reasonable to ask what possible benefit could come from such apparent violence? What is wrong with the ground I stand on? Why strike at the place where I connect as a person? Kidd had been comfortable in her marriage. Reevaluating it and questioning her investment in it struck deep.

For people of faith emotional pain serves as a catalyst for greater spiritual maturity. While cold stoicism has little or no spiritual value, the ability to put our emotions into perspective indicates real spiritual growth. "One of John of the Cross' most important contributions to the history of Christian spirituality is to give a necessary and positive value to experiences of inner frustration and paralysis…They have to be faced, but rightly understood and used, they become a means of growth."[13] Kidd's reinvestment in her marriage is a case in point. Emotional frustration had plagued her during months of silent waiting for God's guidance. In some imperceptible way the months simultaneously brought her closer to God and to her husband. As her pain and confusion decreased, she began to notice her husband's long-suffering presence. Turning her attention from herself to her loving husband woke her, as if from a dream. Finally the direction was clear. Kidd rearranged her priorities, recommitted to her husband and family, and emerged humbly grateful from the ordeal.

Faithful people search urgently for the spiritual potential within emotional pain. Believing in God's love for them arms them to endure the pain. Spiritual maturity may coincide with faith that has undergone trial, but that is not their main concern. Remaining focused on God and refusing to focus on self opens spiritual space within them. They discover greater compassion and generosity there. With matter-of-fact wisdom, Ruth Burrows describes the effect. She says, "Sooner or later each of us has to learn to put up with painful emotions, pay little attention to them, and get on with what we have to do, attending to our neighbors' welfare, putting all our trust in God."[14] Where else could we validly place our trust?

Loss of identity, even a false ego identity, shakes us. Discovering inner contradictions, personal weaknesses, and emotional pain heightens our alarm. Midlife calls into question all that we have previously taken for granted. Without faith, we stand alone on uncertain ground. With faith, and with openness to God, we proceed. Narratives of contemplatives who have persevered in faith shed some light on the terrain. Drawing spiritual wisdom from their experiences strengthens us for the journey and extends hope for a better life beyond.

Anxiety

"I am perhaps at a turning point in my spiritual life: perhaps slowly coming to a point of maturation and the resolution of doubts and the forgetting of fears."[15] Thomas Merton, the well-known Trappist monk and spiritual writer, made this declaration at age forty-six. The scenario of Merton's life features numerous turning points, but this particular one was conclusive. After being orphaned in his teens and drifting through his early twenties, Merton entered the Trappist monastery of Our Lady of Gethsemane, near Louisville, Kentucky. There, coincidentally, he would later meet Matthew Kelty, another spiritual pilgrim and soul mate. Silence, solitude, and withdrawal from the world heavily accented the early years of Merton's monastic life. He prayed, worked, studied, and wrote—externally, he was a model Trappist monk. Internally, however, personal doubts and fears smoldered.

By midlife, Merton wrestled with an increasingly intense desire for solitude countered by an equally intense concern for the world. Both sides of his dilemma stretched the boundaries of Trappist life. He hounded the abbot for permission to live as a hermit, and he wrote political essays that made the Federal Bureau of Investigation suspicious of him. The majority of monks do not behave this way. Consequently, for the most part he suffered his inner struggle alone. In his journals he describes being dazed, desperate, frustrated, and defeated, undergoing "moments of unspeakable anguish and tension."[16] Of course, there were also periods of great joy, and those familiar with Merton's life know how powerfully the tension between the poles of his paradox played out.

The turning point Merton mentions at age forty-six had to do with his decision to write an essay for *The Catholic Worker* called "War Madness." The essay condemned the malicious frenzy that characterized the Cold War years and fueled the nuclear arms race. In it, Merton came forward as a passionate advocate for disarmament and peace. The essay marked the beginning of a stream of social and political critiques that would provoke the disapproval of Trappist censors and the wrath of military and political powers. Yet somehow the decision to take public stands on such issues as war and racism brought him peace.

Merton's social and political writing grew out of twenty years of contemplation. This man applied his brilliant mind to the realities of his time as ardently as he committed himself to contemplative prayer. Reading about the destructive forces at work in the world inflamed his heart steeped in prayer. He could not remain silent and be true to himself and to God. He anguished over the devastating effects of racism and war, and he was compelled to speak out against them. His political stands themselves engendered deep divisions, even while they urged unity and peace. Nevertheless, he grew in the conviction that his individual vocation included both solitary life and political advocacy. He said, "I am happy that I have turned a corner, perhaps the last corner of my life. [I have a] sense of abandon and home-going joy."[17]

Sandra Cronk comments on her work with other midlife people who are going through similar wrenching experiences. She says, "I have met deeply religious, highly gifted, and very sensitive people who feared, in the midst of their dark night journeys, that they would burn up through spontaneous combustion, be destroyed by mechanical monsters, or be shot…Each discovered a new, more joyous and integrated life on the other side of the experience."[18] Of course, it makes sense for people in crisis to express fear and even terror. In the midst of their experience they cannot foresee its outcome. They sense that they will be changed by decisions they make and actions they take, but they cannot tell how. The factor of the unknown at play in their lives can have excruciating, but ultimately purifying, effects on them.

Powerlessness

Merton knew that taking public stands on politically and socially volatile issues would ignite potent reactions, both from his order and from influential people who benefited from the status quo. His courageous decision to speak out anticipated the battles that might ensue. He even expressed willingness to deal directly with whatever negative responses his writings might bring. He was so convinced that taking stands against destructive forces flowed from the heart of Christianity that he accepted any consequences. The freedom, peace, and joy that followed affirmed his decision and prepared him for what would come next.

What Merton did not anticipate was the vehemence with which the censors in his order came down upon him. Because of their religious authority over him, they represented an immovable obstacle to the publication of his work. Their refusal to let him publish his critical essays rendered Merton powerless to fight against the real malice he saw in society. Once he had awakened to the enormous destructive power of nuclear arms in particular, he felt duty bound to use his formidable literary might to prevent their proliferation and potential use. The censors' emphatic prohibition against publishing his essays devastated him.

In his journal, Merton refers to the buildup of nuclear arms as the greatest moral crisis in the history of man. He is outraged at the fact that "there is a definite policy of the Cistercian Order to impede and obstruct every expression of concern, every opinion in published written form that has reference to this crisis." Arguing with superiors only hardened their resistance. Merton found that attempts to persuade them to reverse their decisions were futile. Asking for reconsideration "was like talking to a wall…total incomprehension and lack of sympathy."[19] They were as intractable as the arms race itself. He realized he could do nothing to change their minds. Confronted with the monumental evil of war, and fired with the desire to deter it, he felt completely powerless to do so.

Although they speak from a fundamentally different context, some contemplatives mention powerlessness as an element in their prayer. In diametrically different circumstances from Merton's, they too find themselves unable to act. Contemplation places them in the presence of God, the Ultimate Good. In

God's presence the truth of the weak human condition becomes clear. In God's presence, human action is not only suspended, it becomes unnecessary. It is God who acts. Michael Casey sees the reality of human powerlessness as an invitation to deeper prayer. He says, "What we need to do is take powerlessness as a basic premise, and use it as a fulcrum to lift our hearts in prayer toward God."[20] Of course we are powerless, in comparison with God. But remaining in God's presence shows us that God, whose infinite power reveals our powerlessness, also infinitely loves us.

Both situations—confrontation with evil and encounter with God—leave the individual powerless. In both cases the person deals with influences beyond his control. Contemplatives can rest in God's presence, knowing that God's goodness will transform their later actions. Individuals confronting evil, if they have faith, can surrender the evil situation to God's greater goodness and humbly accept their own inability to change it. Whether the evil is nuclear, political, social, or personal, humans can do no more than to admit their powerlessness against it, and to remain in the situation, if necessary, surrendered to God's invisible presence there.

To his credit, Merton maintained a stance of obedience toward the powers of his order, even though their decisions frustrated and confounded him. He railed against them to God in prayer. He suffered inner anguish and begged God for relief. His passionate nature and keen intelligence exacerbated his frustration. Still, his writings disclose that in this and in other crises of his life, Merton faithfully brought his weakness before the face of God. In God he found rest, and, eventually, peace.

Dependence

At midlife, Merton turned a corner mentally and spiritually. Concern about the social and political issues of his time opened him mentally to the whole world. The global and cosmic implications of the issues opened him spiritually to all people, and to God who loves and cares for all people. At the same time, however, another aspect of Merton's life moved in a different direction. He began to experience the physical aches and pains of the middle years, and to struggle with what would become chronic medical conditions. Just when he seemed to have found God's infinite plan for his intellectual and spiritual life, he was forced to deal with the limitations of his body. The persistent need to address these annoying symptoms seemed unfair. He wrote, "I am nearly forty-eight…I am still too young mentally to be in the least patient with any sign of age. My impatience is felt as an upheaval of resentment, disgust, depression."[21]

Merton's reactions to signs of age sound familiar to anyone who inhabits a midlife body. By midlife, we have seen our families mature, we have arrived at the peak of our careers, we have finely honed our intellectual and practical abilities. We seem to be within reach of goals we have cherished for half a lifetime. Yet it is often at this most auspicious time that minor but irritating physical symptoms begin to appear. Doctor's appointments materialize out of nowhere on our calendars. Medicines and their side effects become facts of life. We need to pace ourselves, to conserve our strength. No wonder the inescapable signs of finitude frustrate and discourage us. At the very time that we feel we have the most to give, we begin to fear that we may fail.

Meanwhile, one more dimension of Merton's life was changing as well. He was asked to oversee the spiritual formation of the novices of the order. He took this responsibility very seriously and gave himself to it wholeheartedly. He diligently prepared conferences and classes that would inspire and inform the novices. As many teachers do, he worried about how to reach his young students, how to move their minds and hearts to God. The importance of the task seemed overwhelming. In addition, others from the monastery community became curious about his classes and wanted to hear Merton's lectures themselves. Their interest honored Merton, but it also weighed on him. What began as a spiritual opportunity became a source of increasing personal pressure. Merton's high expectations of himself were multiplied by the expectations of others. He describes obsessively overpreparing and still being dissatisfied with his work.

As always, Merton surrendered his weaknesses to God in prayer. He wrote, "In everything I have come to feel more than ever my need for grace, my total dependence on God, my helplessness without his special intervention, which I may need at any moment. Never has this been so clear to me. Perhaps it was never before as true as now."[22] The confluence of cosmic concerns and human limitations vividly reminded Merton of his complete dependence on God, who cares tenderly and perfectly about both. By his own efforts, Merton could not reconcile the distance between the two extremes. Only God's infinite perspective could encompass and make coherent sense of them. The desire to align his own vision with the divine perspective brought him to prayer.

In his book, *Silence on Fire*, William Shannon comments on the correlation between dependence upon God and contemplative prayer. He writes, "The two poles of contemplative spirituality are these: God as the Ground of love, and prayer as awareness of this. They flow from a fundamental human intuition of being totally and radically dependent upon God."[23] Many factors can remind us of our dependence on God: undeniable signs of age, impenetrable world problems, and the management of our own expectations and those of others, to name a few. Aware of these factors, Shannon points out, "The very experience of my dependence is simultaneously an experience of the God on whom I totally depend."[24] Shifting our attention away from our own dependent state and directing it toward the God on whom we rely transforms our uncertain attitude into fervent prayer.

Merton spent his later years living in a hermitage on the monastery grounds at Gethsemane. The extended time for silence and solitude that the hermitage afforded brought him inner freedom and peace. Although the monastery in which he had lived for decades profoundly appreciated silence and contemplation, the hermitage provided virtually unlimited expanses of both. His prayer became less wordy and more receptive. Alone with God for long periods of time, he could readily admit his need for God and humbly accept God's loving care. Rather than provoking fear, radical dependence upon God sustained him. In fact, dependence upon God became the greatest security he had ever known.

Absence

For someone like Merton, who has experienced the anxiety that accompanies feelings of powerlessness and dependence, the constant reassurance of God's presence is an underlying necessity. Fortunately, the journals of Merton's later years reflect his real enjoyment of God's presence, especially in his hermitage home and in the nature that surrounded him. Relying on the love and mercy of God put Merton in a position of ultimate security, where there is no fear. Not everyone is as fortunate as he was, however. At midlife some faithful people feel far away from the God on whom they depend. There can be no more threatening experience than to know one's dependence upon God, and then to sense that God is gone.

Speaking from a human standpoint, psychologist Mark Gerzon describes the plight of those who suffer this way. He says, "In the second half of life, it is common to experience feelings of dissatisfaction, alienation and emptiness…We feel inexplicably lost or, more precisely, abandoned."[25] Because the rigors of midlife occur so uniquely in each person, they seem to separate us from each other. One person suffers job dissatisfaction, another experiences broken relationships. One hurts physically, another psychologically. The fact that midlife leaves few people untouched implies that the very ones to whom we ordinarily look for support in our difficulties may be struggling themselves. Without their understanding and encouragement, the impact of our own predicament becomes stronger. When the people we most need least understand, we are in real trouble.

The spiritual analogy to this human phenomenon is the elusiveness of God's presence during our time of need. If we are faithful, we have confidently relied on God's help thus far. During times of crisis especially, we want to be held and nurtured by our loving God. How is it that our time of deepest need sometimes coincides with a sense of God's inscrutable absence? Being less sure of God's presence leaves us feeling bereft of the reassuring comfort we usually find in God. What a time for God to leave!

Thomas Keating explains how this trial may work toward our spiritual good. He says, "The withdrawal of God's felt presence is meant to increase our faith, and without the withdrawal of that sensible presence we remain on a shallow level."[26] Common sense tells us that it is easy to believe when God is near. What it does not tell us is that our faith deepens only when God disappears. Apparent abandonment by God sharpens our need. Our prayer in abandonment comes from the deepest levels of our being. We cry out to God for help, setting no conditions and making no claims. Arrogant attitudes and proud postures vanish. We have nowhere else to turn.

Because God is loving, he does not leave us in this state longer than we can bear. But when God returns, it is as ever more unfathomable Mystery. The God who returns after we have felt abandoned is not the God we took for granted when we were comfortable and secure. This God is infinitely beyond our expectations and demands and still comes to us in our deepest need. Receiving God at that level heals us and makes us whole. We know now for sure that no crisis, however desperate, can separate us from the love of God. Peace and acceptance follow, even though understanding fails.

Merton describes his growing sense of inner peace in his later journals. He writes, "Vigil of my fiftieth birthday. A bright, snowy afternoon, delicate blue clouds of snow blowing down from frozen trees…I thank God for the present, not for myself in the present, but for the present which is his, and in him."[27] Merton lets go of the past and of all anxieties. Asking no questions, he enjoys the presence of God. Living in deep faith, he is truly happy.

Emptiness

Among the experiential signs common to people in crisis and in contemplation is a feeling of inner emptiness. In both contexts people feel that they have little or nothing within them that adequately matches the situation. In crisis, they have no means of coping with the problem that confronts them. In contemplation, they have no resources that correspond with the presence of God. Feeling empty is a natural reaction to experiences that could potentially overwhelm us. Rather than being a liability, however, emptiness may offer the best condition for enduring crisis and for remaining contemplatively present to God. Although uncomfortable, emptiness suggests the defenseless stance, the simplified mind, and the purified heart that enable us to benefit spiritually from emotionally intimidating experiences.

Perhaps the most sobering human experience occurs when we become aware of the fact that we will die. Accepting the inevitability of death requires the highest degree of personal and spiritual maturity. One person who eloquently shared this experience is Cardinal Joseph Bernardin of Chicago. In his mid-sixties, Bernardin suffered two tragic disruptions to his life: false accusation of sexual misconduct and the diagnosis of terminal cancer. He describes his inner reactions to these life-altering experiences in his final book, *The Gift of Peace*.

Reflecting on the ordeal of false accusation and its subsequent withdrawal, Bernardin writes, "I began 1995 as a liberated man. A great weight had been lifted from my shoulders, and I felt freer than ever before."[28] After the accusation was withdrawn Bernardin went to visit his accuser, to offer him forgiveness. The accusation, the investigation, and the final exoneration had taken the better part of a year. He recalls, "During those months I emptied myself more than I ever had so that God could take over." As a man of deep prayer, Bernardin realized that there was little he could do when falsely accused other than emptying himself. He emptied himself of rage over the injustice of the accusation, and of anxiety about how the case might proceed. Most strikingly, he emptied himself of the impulse to take revenge on his accuser. Through this most trying period of his life, emptying himself so that God could come in became his habitual spiritual exercise.

Although the process of deliberate self-emptying carries no predictable results, the effect it had on Bernardin was the expansion of inner freedom. By the time the accusation was withdrawn, he felt able to forgive his accuser and to make a symbolic gesture of reconciliation by visiting him in person. The spiritual courage and strength for his generous act could only come from faithful prayer. Speaking of the purifying effects of such prayer, Carmelite Vilma Seelaus says that in it, "God makes room for God."[29] Notice that when we show willingness to empty ourselves, it is God who takes over. God makes the space for spiritual transformation to take place. At the emotional level the space feels like emptiness; spiritually it represents the influx of God.

Bernardin had been ordained auxiliary bishop of Atlanta at age thirty-eight, at that time the youngest bishop in the United States. By age forty-two he became Archbishop of Cincinnati, and by age fifty-five he became Cardinal Archbishop of Chicago. He served admirably as President of the National Conference of Catholic Bishops, and on behalf of the bishops wrote some of the most persuasive pastoral letters of his time. He stood as a wise and respected figure in American Catholicism. It is one of the dramatic ironies of the spiritual life that a man who fully deserved to count his accomplishments with pride would empty himself so willingly at the most crucial moment. Perhaps it is this humble action, more than any ecclesiastical honor, which truly defines the man.

Abyss

Working with the elderly in nursing home settings, Margaret Guenther, the Episcopal priest mentioned earlier, developed a rather tolerant attitude toward the reality of death. With mild amusement she says, "Our death is inevitable. Mere living is like involuntary participation in a spiritual Lamaze class, preparing us for the final great passage."[30] It is possible that on the day she wrote that, Guenther was feeling more indestructible than usual. People who are healthy, strong, involved, and productive frequently express calm acceptance of their theoretical finitude. They treat it like a problem in basic math and move on. But Guenther admits, "Most of the time I am able to ignore my intuitive flashes of my own impending death, but at odd times I am suffused with an acute awareness of it."

The times of acute awareness are the ones that matter spiritually. As I write this, the story is being told of an eleven-year-old Boy Scout who wandered off from his campsite and walked five miles downstream in the wilderness of the mountains in Utah. Thousands of volunteer rescue workers searched round the clock for him in the deserted area, and after four days and nights they were beginning to lose hope of finding him. Miraculously, one rescuer finally stumbled upon him in an abandoned canyon. The rescuer identified the boy and returned him safely to his parents. In press conferences following the event the parents, who must be people of great faith, expressed their thanks to God and to all those who helped find their son. The distraught mother tried to explain, "We had just about given up hope of ever seeing him alive again," and then broke down.

Stories of miraculous rescues, unexplained cures, and near-death experiences acquaint us with the fragility of life. Chillingly, they bring home to us the absolute value of every day, every person. Ludwig Heyde puts this message into philosophical terms. He says, "Contingent being bears non-being within it. Every moment of its existence it hangs above the abyss of nothingness."[31] Because we are all contingent beings, because none of us sustains our own being in existence, we all hang above the same allegorical abyss; but the vicissitudes of midlife may bring the abyss into clearer focus. Warnings about our finitude add urgency to some of our life goals. We care more than ever about things like the forgiveness of wrongs, the giving of peace, the expression of love. These sometimes deferred goals suddenly become immediate and imperative. "The second half of life, and most particularly the approach of death, brings a narrowing of the circle, a falling away of the extraneous."[32] And, we might add, the emergence into bright clarity of what is most important in our lives.

Ordinary modes of operating cannot accommodate this degree of existential awareness. That is exactly why midlife awareness throws us drastically outside of our comfort zone. Midlife puts what is essential at the forefront of our consciousness, whether or not we are inclined to deal with it. The quality of our relationships, the true value of our accomplishments, our faults, and our regrets—all of these matters immediately concern us. We want to resolve them while there is still time. Hollis says that at midlife, "We return again and again to the edge of the abyss, the cracking ice beneath our feet, poised above whatever it is we have most sought to avoid."[33] What we do not realize is that until we give essential things the attention they deserve, they will continue to haunt us.

For example, when Cardinal Bernardin gave reporters the news of his terminal diagnosis, one of them asked whether he had anything special he wanted to accomplish during the time he had left. After mentioning his desire to be with friends and family, he realized that although he was dying he had within his power the opportunity to communicate his last spiritual message to his people. He said, "Finally, the answer that was eluding me surfaced in my mind. It was so simple that I had not yet been able to put it into words. I told the media that probably the most important thing I could do for the people of the Archdiocese— and everyone of good will—would be so show them how I prepare for death."[34]

By modeling how to prepare for death, Bernardin taught the most moving lesson of his life. He accepted his impending death with total confidence in the next life. He spent much of his remaining time ministering to fellow cancer patients, offering them spiritual support in their shared journey. He used his diminishing energy to attend diocesan events, to continue to reach out to people both literally and figuratively. He demonstrated that, paradoxically, we prepare for death by truly living life. By accessing stores of courage and generosity that are not usually available to us, we live the very best quality of life. If we live like this, we will be at peace with ourselves and others. Then indeed death has no sting.

New Life

"It is quite clear now that I will not be alive in the spring. But I will soon experience new life in a different way."[35] Cardinal Bernardin wrote these words of faith a few months before he died. Those who were close to him at that time say he maintained a spirit of deep calm and equanimity. When the end drew near he lived, as many dying people do, less in this world and more in the next. Coming to terms with absolutes like life and death strengthens our spiritual faculties. It draws us away from the petty and trivial and orients us toward the most ultimate reality we can imagine. It offers us, on the other side of the abyss, a life that transcends death, a life that is eternal.

If we rise to the midlife challenge of dealing with essential issues in honesty and humility, we can move on in the second half of life with unshakeable faith. Christians believe that the dying and rising of Jesus make it possible for us also to die and then rise. What is truly amazing, though, is the fact that this paschal mystery is available to us not only at the end of our lives, but every day of our lives and every moment. The death we undergo at midlife, for example, is not physical death, but the death of superficiality and falsity. As we have seen in the stories of Merton,

Bernardin, and others, personal crisis strips away all that is nonessential in us and brings us into closer intimacy with God.

William Shannon describes the kind of prayer by which we move away from desperate anxiety and toward new life. He calls it "precarious prayer," taken from the Latin word *preces*, which means "begging" or "beseeching." Shannon assumes that deep prayer comes from profound need, and that the person who turns to God in crisis can pray only that way. Describing this type of prayer he says, "It suggests relating to God in a condition of instability, risk, total vulnerability. The one who prays is, if you will, in the constant state of existential precariousness. One is conscious of living continually on the edge of nothingness, yet equally conscious of being kept from falling into the abyss by the sustaining hand of God."[36] Life offers us continual opportunities for precarious prayer, but at times we are more aware of the need for it than others. When reporters asked the eleven-year-old Boy Scout wandering in the Utah wilderness what he did when he first realized he was lost, he said, "I prayed." We can only imagine the intensity of his prayer.

Most of us will be blessed with long and happy lives. If, however, there are moments that make us more aware than usual of the shortness of life, these same moments also reveal the nearness of God. Realizing, even if only for a moment, that this life spills over into eternity gives it inestimable value. "Death is what gives our lives a sense of urgency and ultimacy," says theologian John Sachs. "Because we have a specific, limited time and space in which to accomplish something, we are forced to take our time and action seriously. What I do or do not do makes a difference…It makes each of us take stock of our lives and ask, 'What have I done, what will I have done with my life?'"[37]

People of faith who ask questions like these are already living out the answers. The very fact that we pause and try to see our lives from the perspective of eternity ensures that we will live from that point on in closer union with the eternal God. Living in conscious union with God makes every moment eternal, perfect, and true. There can be no greater liberation and no greater peace.

5
Response

When we encounter the Absolute, whether in personal crisis or in contemplation, we stop short. Time stands still, and ordinary modes of operating fail. We face something or someone we can neither control nor avoid. We fall back on our own limited resources, which soon evaporate. Temporarily suspended, we feel we can do little or nothing to respond. It is precisely at that moment, however, that our response becomes quintessentially important. If by an act of faith we assent to the presence of God within the inescapable present, that very act unites us with God at that moment. If by an act of surrender we consent to live through the experience in union with God, that nearly imperceptible act satisfies perfectly.

Each person responds to an Absolute encounter uniquely. One admits that a personal relationship has ended badly and seeks forgiveness in God's presence. Another accepts physical illness and finds in God the help to endure it gracefully. A third passes through a crisis of faith and lets the divine break into daily life. The way each person responds to the encounter marks that person as an individual. No one else encounters the Absolute in exactly the same way, nor does any other person respond identically. But if faith initiates the response and surrender follows, all will find themselves united with God in the process.

This chapter traces the responses of two people whose life stories illustrate acts of faith and surrender. British author C. S. Lewis' biography describes the incremental stages of his religious conversion. The life of Edith Stein, the German Jewish woman who became a Carmelite saint, does the same. May their stories and others like them suggest ways of responding in crisis or in contemplation that allow us to grow in union with God.

RESPONSE

Choice

The mother of British writer C. S. Lewis died when he was nine years old. Like Gerald May, whose story appeared earlier, Lewis implicitly blamed God for the loss. By the age of thirteen he wandered away from his childhood faith and became darkly pessimistic. Classical Greek and Latin texts, Wagnerian music, and German idealistic philosophy occupied him during adolescence and young adulthood. He excelled as a student at Oxford University and became Fellow and Tutor of English Literature there for thirty years. Although he had considered the matter closed, the question of God returned to trouble him seriously during his early years as a professor.

In his book *Surprised by Joy*, Lewis compares God's pursuit of him to a game of chess. He confesses to using tactics of skepticism and cynicism to dodge God's advance. With subtle arguments and metaphysical questions, he stalled for time. With patient persistence, God cornered him in an inextricable checkmate. The endgame occurred in London one day while Lewis was riding on the top of a double-decker bus. Suddenly he understood that it was God he was keeping at bay rather than some inconsequential troublesome thought. There was no way he could escape this Adversary. He reports nevertheless that after he had exhausted all alternatives, God dealt with him most respectfully.

Lewis writes, "The odd thing was that before God closed in on me, I was in fact offered what now appears to be a moment of wholly free choice."[1] The choice, of course, was whether or not he would acknowledge the reality of God. Although it appeared to be simple, for Lewis the choice was momentous. It would determine the future direction of his life. Still God left the decision entirely up to him. Lewis says, "This came closer to being a perfectly free act than most that I have ever done." Ultimately he chose in favor of God, but not before delaying a little longer.

The bombardment of advertising aimed at us relentlessly suggests the subtle but invaluable capacity we have for choice.

Advertisers know that we may choose their product or another; we may opt to purchase or to postpone. They use every motivation available to attract our choice, often creating imaginary scenarios that promise immediate physical or sensual gratification if we select their products. When the choice concerns everyday consumer items, it carries little weight and we give it little thought. If it involves the purchase of a home or a car, we pay much closer attention. We question and compare; we seek advice and give our options careful consideration. If the decision involves the future direction of our lives, such as the choice of a spouse, a career, or a vocation, the stakes escalate even higher.

Lewis' choice of whether or not to acknowledge the reality of God falls into the third and most important category. John Crosby would compare it to Kierkegaard's notion of a fundamental option, a choice or decision that determines the direction of all future decisions. A fundamental option regarding God or any other Absolute reality elevates us by connecting our capacity to choose with a totally transcendent object. Crosby says, "There are experiences of being raised above myself, of being empowered by some source outside of myself," and in those rare instances, "a single free act can reorient my whole life."[2] Notice that Crosby places the fundamental option in a passive or receptive context of "being raised" or "being empowered." His careful phrasing hints at the fact that we do not initiate fundamental options; they confront us. By their very nature, they take us beyond ourselves. The fact that we realize their significance invests them with even greater worth.

Lewis' account of his encounter with God acknowledges God's initiative while preserving his own capacity for free choice. Even though it was God who closed in on him, Lewis remained free to choose his response. Perhaps the same sort of thing happens when we find ourselves in personal crisis. We do not choose the nature or circumstances of the crisis. If we did, the situation would not constitute a crisis. The involuntary nature of crisis thrusts us into a forced choice position about something of consequence: our family, our integrity, our reputation, our beliefs. In issues such as these, our response matters deeply.

Ruth Burrows mentions some of the personal factors that come into play in situations of significant choice. Recognizing that at critical times when we most need to choose wisely we are least inclined to do so, she says, "We have one dynamism of choice. That dynamism must be controlled, concentrated, otherwise it ceases to be dynamic…We must decide what we really want and concentrate on that."[3] When the choice is insignificant, it presents no problem. When it asks us to identify what we really want, and to put everything we have and are behind our selection, something within us spontaneously rebels. To choose well and remain faithful to our choice, we must concentrate. We must faithfully discipline our tendency to consider other options. The capacity for a self-imposed moratorium flows from our dignity as persons. We are capable of making a full and deliberate commitment, but doing so challenges us at the deepest levels. Responding to that challenge by choosing well maximizes our potential as human beings and moves us toward fuller, more meaningful life.

An example may help to show the dynamics involved in a serious choice. Let us imagine a family with nearly grown children. When the parents, whom we will call Joe and Anne, are just beginning to consider their empty nest, a tragic accident presents them with a decision that will influence the rest of their lives. A car crash takes the lives of Joe's brother and sister-in-law, and Joe and Anne face the possibility of becoming responsible for their young children. Joe and Anne are generous people, and they want to do everything they can to welcome the children into their family and to console them for their loss. However, they also realize the multitude of implications that option entails. Are they too old to parent young children? Will the children be able to adjust? The generous decision to accept the challenges presented by the tragic loss seems to come from beyond them. On their own, they would never attempt it, yet they feel somehow empowered to do the only thing that they know is right. Relying on a power greater than themselves, they respond.

Because Joe and Anne are faithful people, they turn to God in this crisis as they do regularly in their lives. It seems clear to them that God will provide for them and the children, although they do not see immediately how this will happen. Their decision to adopt the children is a decision made in faith, and they hope for God's guidance as they work out its details. Michael Casey seems to be describing a faith perspective like theirs when he says, "There is a crucial point in which a decision has to be taken concerning who is in charge. If it is to be God, then back off. *Let God act.*"[4] Crises like Joe and Anne's would cause anyone to wonder who is in charge. If they decide that God is in charge, the only option that follows is to let God act. Rather than burdening themselves with worries and fears, they begin to operate on a more transcendent level, relying on God in all things.

Although the single free act we have been considering is made once and for all—the choice by Lewis to believe in God, the decision by Joe and Anne to adopt the children—it needs to be sustained over time. Burrows affirms the necessity for remaining faithful to such commitments. She says, "We must make up our minds once for all, renewing the decision countless times daily, hourly, that we shall let God have everything he wants. That we shall trust him."[5] If any single free act is going to reorient our whole lives, there could be none greater than this.

Finite Meets Infinite

When Joe and Anne make the altruistic choice of adopting the orphaned children, they are in a state of shock themselves. Because the tragic accident that took his brother's life was caused by another driver and not by his brother's negligence, Joe realizes that the same thing might have happened to him. He experiences the survivor's complex reaction of grief for the loss of his brother mixed with gratitude for his own remaining life.

RESPONSE

Sensing that he could have died in similar random circumstances makes every moment of his life more meaningful and more precious. Burrows expresses the power of such realizations, which are often linked to the unavoidable vicissitudes of midlife. She says, "Bereavement, disappointment, failure, old age…and countless other common human experiences engulf us…All of them confront us with our finitude, raise fundamental questions of human existence, and contain a challenge to accept our human vocation."[6]

Our human vocation is both noble and mysterious. We feel called to something or someone beyond ourselves, but we do not know specifically toward whom or what we are called. We can only respond by acts of faith. C. S. Lewis found himself drawn toward an act of faith, but not compelled to make it. He was drawn by God to acknowledge God while his freedom to do so remained intact. Yet he also felt that the power drawing him far outweighed his ability to resist. With mild irony he asks, "How could the initiative be on my side?…If Shakespeare and Hamlet should ever meet, it must be Shakespeare's doing." Certainly, Lewis knew amiable agnostics who talked about man's search for God, but he says, "They might as well have talked about the mouse's search for the cat."[7] In other words, when God approaches, our limited ability to choose meets God's unlimited power to attract us. Could the metaphorical chess match be rigged?

Joe and Anne could have avoided their apparently inescapable responsibility. They could have pointed to their age or health or financial status as valid reasons to decline. They could have suggested younger, less obligated foster parents as being more suitable. They could have chosen to ignore the family's needs and to fulfill their cherished dreams of carefree and well-deserved retirement. Because they are people of faith, however, larger issues come into play. They believe that God, who is ultimate generosity, is calling them to extraordinary generosity. James Hollis suggests that people in their situation see their choice as "an invitation to enlarged consciousness and, with that, to some possibility of meaning." Like other mature, responsible people they may recognize that "this is the life we get, not another. This one is short, for real. It is precisely its finitude which brings choice home, makes some freedom possible and decisiveness necessary."[8]

In crisis, it is likely that people might feel stumped or defeated by forces beyond their control. If another couple in circumstances similar to Joe and Anne's were to decide to adopt the children, they might do so with grim determination or a cynical spirit. It would be understandable if they felt cheated out of the idyllic future they had envisioned for themselves. They might harbor unconscious resentment toward the children or toward the fate that brought them together, and that attitude might further color the working out of their lives. If they think they have only themselves and their limited resources to fall back on, they may feel tested beyond their endurance or even cruelly trapped.

Seeing crisis in a context of faith offers broader insights into its potential. It provides the enlarged consciousness Hollis suggests. Seeing crisis as a case in which our own finite abilities must turn to God's infinite strength opens up transcendent possibilities within the crisis and within us. When the divine approaches the human, as God approached Lewis in his crisis of faith, the human is liable to recoil. Who could feel adequate when measured against the immeasurable? Admitting that we may be in the presence of the Infinite throws our finite limits into stark relief. It pokes holes in our proud pretensions. As Ludwig Heyde says, acknowledging our finitude implies accepting "the nothingness that surrounds every existence." It exposes all hidden assumptions about our own omnipotence. He adds, "The presence of the essential—of God—can only be understood when…finitude is truly recognized as finite, and not in a concealed way made into something absolute."[9] No being other than God evokes such a response in us. No other apprehension about our condition conveys more truth.

When viewed in the light of faith, the interplay between human finitude and divine infinity can be seen as liberating rather than defeating. When we act in faith the world suddenly becomes the universe, and our spirits expand accordingly. Earlier in his philosophical explorations, C.S. Lewis had toyed with the notion of an inexorable Fate and that hypothetical notion terrified him. He wanted at all costs to avoid meeting it. He describes himself as "kicking, struggling, resentful, and darting his eyes in every direction for a chance of escape." How well we recognize Lewis' all too human reactions. Fortunately, he somehow also perceived the possibility of a loving, caring God who would be even greater than any impersonal Fate. When he finally cast his lot with that God, he experienced immediate release. Looking back years later at God's patience with him he admits, "The hardness of God is kinder than the softness of men, and his compulsion is our liberation."[10]

Let us imagine that Joe and Anne make their generous decision and in doing so experience a similar liberation. Their one simple decision made in faith simultaneously opens the unfathomable love of God more fully to them. Aligning our will with the will of God as Joe and Anne hope to do lets God act through us, and God always acts with loving kindness. That principle does not imply that Joe and Anne will begin exhibiting superhuman powers or that the new life they build with the children will be without trials. It does imply that a loving, caring God will encompass their human limitations and that they will negotiate their trials in ongoing faith.

Similarly, Lewis would repeat the act of faith begun in the moment on the double-decker bus as his conversion proceeded. Remaining the intellectual that he was, he would continue to pursue paths of inquiry and exploration; but he would do so in a spirit of confident freedom, even playfulness. His delightful *Chronicles of Narnia*, written for children, and his fanciful *Screwtape Letters*, written for searchers like himself, worked out many of his own metaphysical curiosities. His profound *Mere Christianity* testified to his maturing faith and humbly offered it to others as an invitation. Like Pascal, who compared his leap of faith to a foolproof wager, Lewis understood that he had nothing to lose and everything to gain by believing.

Divine Initiative

Early on in this study we learned that involuntary change sometimes precipitates crisis. The involuntary quality of some changes takes us by surprise, thwarts our plans, and squanders our resources. It contradicts the notion that we are masters of our own fortunes. Analogously, it leads to the logical deduction that if we are not masters, then there must be someone else who is master. The intuition of the existence of this vague, amorphous Someone entails both promising and threatening possibilities at the same time. Only when the Someone begins to assert itself can we discern its true nature. Until then we hang suspended, unsure of what will follow.

Lewis found himself somewhat involuntarily pursued by God. He described God's approach as a process by which God "closed in" on him. He realized the significance of the choice God presented to him and its implications for the rest of his life. In his spiritual autobiography he says, "The real issue was that if you seriously believed in God, a wholly new situation developed."[11] Believing in God would turn over the initiative to God not just at that moment, but as a consciously chosen pattern for life. It was beyond Lewis' ability to fully execute such an important decision. The very power for him to make an act of faith came from God. Heyde says, "Faith is not created by the human being, but it is received, for nothing, it is grace."[12] Divine initiative is utterly gratuitous and it is always benevolent, although we do not necessarily perceive these attributes when God first acts in our lives.

We see now the value of Ignatius' method for the discernment of spirits. Ignatius assumes that because we are spiritual beings we are open to the influences of spiritual powers, for better or for worse. He warns us to be cautious about following a spiritual influence without first interrogating its intent. We do that by weighing the effects of the spirit's action within us. If the spirit uplifts us, increasing our faith, hope, and love, then it comes from God. If the opposite is true, the source is evil. The gentle and delicate art of discernment of spirits is perfectly suited to our choice of response to situations beyond our control, whether they are times of personal crisis or moments of encounter with God.

God respected Lewis' freedom, but also continued to advance. Lewis frantically weighed the effect of God's approach on his spirit. Was this merely "the God of popular religion," for which he had only contempt? Or was this indeed the living God? Could he dare to trust, or should he flee? There was no time left for questioning. He realized, "I was to be allowed to play at philosophy no longer…My adversary waived the point…He only said, 'I am the Lord'; 'I am that I am'; 'I am.'"[13] There was nothing more to say; nor was there anything for Lewis to do. His role was simply to affirm the presence of God in faith. That single free act reoriented his whole life.

Spiritual writers agree that valid religious experiences originate in God, not in us. We play a cooperative role in the drama, learning our lines along the way. When Hamlet encounters Shakespeare, as Lewis' metaphor suggests, it is Hamlet who takes direction. When we encounter God, we do best to affirm the reality humbly and simply. Describing this sort of ongoing act of faith in God, Burrows says, "True faith never takes its gaze off reality, seeking in it always the face of God which it *knows* is there."[14] Believing in God unites us with God and acknowledges the mysterious goodness of union with God, even when there is abundant evidence to the contrary in the practical realm. In faith, "human activity diminishes and God takes the initiative…As faith is the medium of access to God, it follows that the greater the faith, the greater the union with him."[15]

Union with God would guide Lewis in his continuing life of faith. As a free gift it brought the peace and security to him that he had previously sought through intellectual effort. Unfortunately, his own questioning had only served to upset and confuse him. Introspection had brought doubt and the temptation to despair. By contrast, faith in God engendered hope. The change transformed Lewis from within. As Vilma Seelaus says, "Only through union with God can we access our deepest self. No amount of inner work on our part brings us there. The deepest part of us is accessible only through a relationship of faith with God. It is God who leads us into the deeper reaches of the human."[16] Before his assent to God, Lewis hardly knew himself, because disturbing questions so disquieted his searching soul. Accepting God and affirming God's constant, abiding presence calmed and steadied him, and it allowed his deepest self to emerge.

Being able to think and choose and act ennobles us as human beings. But these abilities can also tempt us to believe that we are the center of reality. That mistaken notion throws all other realities out of perspective and weakens our ability to cope with persons and situations that make no sense to us or defy our intentions. The most intelligent, most competent among us may be most vulnerable in these cases, because they are accustomed to being in charge. The loss of their effectiveness exposed by crisis situations could so disarm them that inner chaos might occur, unless they can envision a divine effectiveness infinitely greater than theirs. Standing still in the midst of potential chaos and yielding the initiative in the situation to God rather than grasping desperately for it themselves may gradually reveal a sense of direction. Then, although practical matters may remain in disarray, their inner being, united with God, can stand firm.

God never intends chaos, and God does not place us in chaotic situations in order to try us. However, when such situations occur, they provide opportunities for us to act in deeper faith. If previously in our life of faith we have allowed God to draw near, we will be more able to trust that God is lovingly present at all times and in all situations regardless of their threatening potential. Believing that takes us beyond the perplexities of immediate events and puts us more directly into relationship with God. United with God, we are able to endure all things.

RESPONSE

Guided by God, we are able to respond to all situations in ways that are genuine and true. We may never be called upon to act heroically, but we will always be able to act rightly. Attuning ourselves ever more finely to the presence of God, we will sense God's initiative and increasingly make it our own.

Tragic events put Joe and Anne into a predicament of forced choice. They searched for some meaning in the heartbreaking loss of innocent loved ones. Because they were people of faith, they were accustomed to discerning God's presence and action in their lives. They knew for certain that God did not inflict meaningless death on their relatives. But because the deaths occurred, they believed that God would lead them to act in the right way in response. They also believed that God would give them the courage and generosity they would need to fulfill the role of foster parents that befell them. Their belief in God's help sustained them; they knew from experience that God is completely good.

Surrender

In his early thirties, Lewis knew that he must choose for or against the God who pursued him. There would be no halfmeasures. "Total surrender, the absolute leap in the dark, were demanded…The demand was not even 'All or nothing.' Now, the demand was simply 'All.'" He describes himself working in his study night after night, trying unsuccessfully to concentrate, and sensing "the steady, unrelenting approach of Him whom I so earnestly desired not to meet. That which I greatly feared had at last come upon me." It was time for him to choose, and he finally did so. "In the Trinity term of 1929 I gave in, and admitted that God was God, and knelt and prayed."[17] His surrender was as total as it was simple. God asked nothing more of him than admitting that God is God. That admission made Lewis' conversion complete.

In Germany only seven years earlier another respected intellectual, teacher, and writer made the same kind of momentous decision. Edith Stein, a brilliant Jewish woman who had devoted herself to the life of the mind, allowed God to enter her heart. The story of Stein's conversion is well known. She had searched in philosophy as Lewis had, and she had failed to find an ultimate truth that could satisfy her. While writing her dissertation in her early twenties, the search for truth had so obsessed her that she came near despair. Describing her inner state at that point she wrote, "It was the first time in my life that I had ever confronted anything that I couldn't master by sheer force of will…Rational arguments didn't help at all. I couldn't cross the street without hoping to be run over or go hiking without wanting to fall so that I wouldn't have to come back alive."[18]

Neither her fine mind nor her strong will could provide Stein with the certainty she desired. Coincidentally, the urgent need for nurses during World War I, which plagued Europe in those years, presented an altruistic purpose for her. The opportunity to give of herself to others in need focused her energies. After volunteering to serve at a military hospital, she wrote to a friend, "My life isn't my own anymore. All my energy belongs to the great undertaking…I offered myself without restriction. If there was anything I wanted, it was to be sent out as soon and as far as possible, preferably to a field hospital on the front."[19] The extravagance of her commitment showed the largeness of her heart. She served for six months caring for wounded soldiers who had contracted infectious diseases and was awarded the medal of valor for her selfless service.

Immediate contact with wounded humanity and daily immersion in life or death battles helped to direct Stein's continuing journey. Her search for truth expanded to include a search for other-centered love, and for a way to commit herself entirely to both. Having fulfilled her time of service in the military, she returned to the university, completed her dissertation *On the Problem of Empathy,* and was awarded the doctoral degree summa cum laude. During those university years, her studies brought her into contact with friends who shared her desire for truth and who found guiding insights in religious literature. One night, while she was staying with friends who had gone out for the evening, she picked up the biography of Teresa of Avila, which she found on a bookshelf in the house. She was captivated by Teresa's story and stayed up all night reading it. She found in Teresa something she had been looking for, a way to truth that leads through love, in Teresa's case, the love of God.

One of her biographers writes, "What Edith Stein found in Teresa's autobiography was the confirmation of her own experience. God is not a God of knowledge, God is love. He does not reveal his mysteries to the deductive intelligence, but to the heart that surrenders itself to him."[20] Stein could see that as a life commitment, Teresa's surrender to God in love far surpassed the search for intellectual truth that had formerly motivated her. Surrender to God in faith would bypass intellectual theories and allow her to give herself totally to God, the source of truth and love. Without informing her family or friends, she resolved to prepare herself for baptism.

Crises of faith challenged Lewis and Stein to surrender to God when they were in their early thirties. Still the pattern of their experience echoes that of many in midlife who perceive in their critical moments a chance to reorient their lives and to surrender to a more transcendent way of being. The surrender that midlife calls for often amounts to relinquishing goals we had previously struggled mightily to attain. The surprise that awaits us on the other side of surrender is the fact that relinquishing those goals, insofar as it becomes clear that they are unattainable, frees us rather than frustrates us. Writing from the perspective of a psychologist of midlife, James Hollis says, "The paradox is that only through relinquishing all that we have sought do we transcend the delusory guarantee of security and identity; all sought, let go. Then, most strangely, surplus of existence floods our heart. Then we move from knowledge of the head, important as it sometimes is, to the wisdom of the heart."[21]

Moving from head to heart implies losing a certain degree of control and renders us more receptive than we may comfortably tolerate being. Especially if we are adept at rational planning and practical execution, we are reluctant to abandon these valuable skills. Only when some form of crisis makes it clear to us that our abilities are inadequate for the situation at hand do we turn to other means. "At some point in the journey, the journeyer comes to realize that the process is larger than he or she is, and an acceptance of this involves a certain passivity."[22] The murkiness of midlife necessitates a certain passivity. Things happen that we do not understand. Inner and outer changes disorient us. Our personal perspective on these matters can make all the difference between a passivity that stems from bitter defeat and one that flows from transcendent faith and hope.

Even if we are tentative about surrendering to God in faith, the slightest move in that direction brings immediate confirmation of our choice. God so delights in our coming closer that divine love meets us more than halfway. Speaking from experience, Carmelite Vilma Seelaus says, "As we surrender to the inflow of divine love, everything in life becomes an access to God and acclimates us for God. Our human failings, psychological limitations, physical infirmities, and other imperfections may continue to be a part of life, but these serve only to deepen humility."[23] If midlife has made our human weaknesses more apparent to us, it may also lead us to greater trust in God's infinite strength. Cultivating an attitude of surrender to God while remaining energetically engaged in midlife realities may set the best course for the remainder of our lives.

Individuation

The process of individuation presents one of the developmental tasks of the middle years. Individuation is a process by which we become who we choose to become as mature individuals, irrespective of influences that may have overshadowed our earlier development. It takes place through a series of conscious, deliberate choices that focus us as persons and move us toward what has become most meaningful for us. Just as unlimited possibilities characterize adolescence, so do more nuanced opportunities characterize midlife. By midlife we have eliminated some of the superficial or trivial fantasies we entertained earlier. We have made choices and established values that define who we are. The more personal and unique our choices, the more they differentiate us from others.

Nothing dramatizes the differences among individual adults more emphatically than the infamous high school reunion. Meeting old friends there, if we decide to attend, shows the radical divergence of our life paths. Some are happily married while others are divorced. Some have remained in the hometown while others have moved continuously. Successes and failures, health and illness, satisfaction and dissatisfaction are all represented. Nostalgia and good humor allow us to review the various paths our lives have taken. Admittedly, circumstances beyond our control created some of the differences among us, but others are the result of our own decisions. Often these occasions allow us to appreciate more deeply the life-directing choices we have made.

Jungian psychologists propose individuation as a model for an adult process of conscious choices leading to a life that is more fully our own and not that of any other person. At best this process highlights our gifts and expresses our values. It brings us to clarity about what is most meaningful to us and it urges us to become increasingly more whole. Earlier we considered the principle that the spirit within us desires meaning, and that through the crises of midlife the spirit can lead us toward greater meaning, even if doing so implies confronting our inner contradictions and addressing issues that were previously closed. We now see that letting the spirit lead us may move us to choices and decisions that differentiate us markedly from others.

Anne Brennan and Janice Brewi allude to this process in their courageous *Passion for Life*. They observe, "Individuation is the process of little by little becoming more whole, more and more my Self…There is no point in life where I can abandon myself or give up on myself."[24] If I am not true to myself, no one else can be. Being true to oneself, while representing courageous choices and bold actions, also separates us from others. In particular, it may separate us from family members and close friends. In fact, individuation may require a rearrangement of the very intimate relationships on which we depend. For that reason, it poses a fearsome challenge.

The life of Edith Stein offers a vivid example of the relational shifts that accompany individuation. Edith was the youngest of eleven children and her father died at the early age of forty-eight. It is understandable that after their father's death the Stein children clung to their mother, and that as the youngest Edith would remain with her mother while others grew up and left home. One friend who knew the family well said, "Her mother was the center of her life; being ready to care for her always took first place."[25] Of all the children, Edith was the most faithful about accompanying her mother to synagogue, and she witnessed there her mother's complete absorption in God. Her mother's mysticism fascinated Edith, but the Jewish faith and traditions of the Stein home did not match her unique call. It was partly in pursuit of a transcendent reality in which she could similarly immerse herself that Edith undertook her long personal and spiritual journey.

Edith's decision to seek baptism caused her mother great pain. Mother and daughter were deeply devoted to each other, and the power of Edith's conversion threatened to separate them at a profound level. While preparing for baptism, Edith would leave the house very early to go to Mass and return thinking that no one knew she had been gone. Years later her mother told a family friend that she always wept bitter tears when she heard the door close, because she knew it had to be Edith going off to church. Edith would never deliberately have provoked her mother's tears. Rather, her friend said, "Edith wanted nothing more than to be a good daughter to her mother, and this remained true after she set out on her appointed path."[26] Edith knew that her approaching baptism would symbolically distance her from her mother, but even at that cost, she felt she must proceed.

The delicate dynamics of individuation accompany the separation of children from their parents, even when the separation involves adult children, or when adult children need to separate psychologically from parents who are gone. Chronological age does not ensure adult choices. Nor do physical changes such as geographic moves accomplish the task of individuation. To individuate the maturing person must acknowledge both the pain of separation and the attraction of the value that motivates the separation. The greater good that attracts us must outweigh the lesser good that holds us back. For example, "Edith had a difficult road right from the start, between the pain she felt at causing her mother suffering and her joy at growing into her authentic life." Nevertheless, her friend concluded that Edith's conversion was authentic because "no matter how threatening the outward circumstances became, she only became freer and larger in spirit. Nothing was able to shake her confidence."[27]

Edith was baptized at the age of thirty-one, but she did not go to the Carmelite monastery until the age of forty-two, even though her desire for the monastic life developed almost simultaneously with her call to conversion. Consideration for her mother delayed the move. Explaining the decision to postpone her departure, Edith wrote, "When I saw my mother for the first time after the baptism, I realized that she couldn't handle another blow for the present." Accordingly, she spent the intervening eleven years in a quiet life of study, teaching, writing, and prayer. At great length the time for Edith to enter Carmel arrived. Recalling the night before she left her home, Edith said, "My mother buried her face in her hands and began to cry...I sat alongside her at the edge of the bed until she sent me off to sleep. But I don't think any one of us got any sleep that night."[28]

Not all experiences of individuation are as wrenching as Edith Stein's was. However, individuation usually entails some pain. Leaving home, choosing a career, taking moral stands, building a marriage, deciding how we will parent our children or accompany our friends—all of these deliberate adult choices separate us from others while they uncover our true identity and establish the foundations for our mature years. Midlife may call one or more of the significant facets of our lives into question.

Reevaluating them during a time of crisis allows us to appreciate their value for us more deeply. In rare cases, we may choose to reset our priorities or adjust our relationships. If doing so brings us closer to our true calling, it can only bring about good for others and for ourselves. "In the end, that summons is our vocation, the calling to become oneself is part and parcel of individuation."[29]

If midlife and its crises contain a subtle summons for us, so too do our moments of contemplation. Contemplative moments, rare and fleeting as they may be, bring us into the presence of God. In God's presence, we are called to ever-greater truth and ever more selfless love. Simply being with God has this effect on us. Likewise, if the choices and decisions that individuate us are authentic, they too will make us more truthful and more loving people. If our choices consistently come from faith and support genuine commitments, they will help us to become freer and more peaceful over time. They will also unite us more closely with God.

Union with Jesus

During the long maturation period between her baptism and her entrance into Carmel, Edith Stein became increasingly united with the person of Jesus. Something pulled her attention especially to his sufferings on the Cross. In her journal she wrote that anyone who belongs to Christ will pass through all of the stages of his life, including the final stages of suffering and death. Perhaps a premonition of the approaching fate of her Jewish countrymen and of her own arrest and subsequent death at Auschwitz led her to this sobering truth. After entering Carmel, when the time came for her to choose a religious name, she took the name Teresa Benedicta of the Cross to remind her of Jesus' love for us demonstrated by his death on the Cross.

Ian Matthew, the British Carmelite, echoes Stein's spiritual insight. He reminds us that Jesus has already undergone any trial or suffering we may endure. His suffering and death epitomize all that is possible in human crisis. Because Jesus understands our pain, and because of his tender love for us, we have every reason to believe that he is closest to us when we are most in need. Matthew says, "Whatever the person may be suffering, Jesus has touched and sanctified that abyss…The suffering of the Son of God, wrecked, mocked, deserted, and Godforsaken, offers a home for everyone's sorrow." Here the divine initiative reaches deeply into the human psyche. Sharing our human nature, Jesus' suffering encompasses all possible human pain. He is "especially associated with the inner pain which bites at the level of spirit."[30] Far from abandoning us in our deepest pain, Jesus makes a home for us there. He offers shelter, compassion, and healing. Ours is only to accept his offer by a simple act of surrender.

The fact that the Son of God wants to be with us, even in our most desperate hours, defies human understanding. When we are in crisis, we would rather be any other place if we possibly could. But it is precisely "through our troubles that we can enter a level of human truth not accessible by any other means. When we identify with Christ crucified, our spiritual life takes on reality and solidity. Strangely, by facing the worst in ourselves we can begin to perceive the glimmer of a hope that is unshakeable."[31] Does it require a crisis for us to be this honest with ourselves? The question is irrelevant. What matters is that, instead of denying our weakness or despising ourselves, we surrender to Jesus, who is lovingly present to us.

By 1938, Hitler's ascendancy made it clear that, like all German Jews, Edith Stein and her family were in great danger. If events unfolded at she feared they might, Hitler would bring great harm to her and to those she loved. She wanted at all costs to spare the Carmelite sisters at Cologne with whom she lived the exposure to punitive measures that her presence there might incur. She escaped to another Carmel at Echt in Holland, where she and the sisters hoped she would be safe. Shortly after arriving in Echt she wrote, "It's clearly God's will that has brought me here—and that is the safest haven of peace…As long as God's will is accomplished in me, I ask for nothing else. It's up to him how long I stay here and what will happen after that; these are things which I don't need to worry about."[32] People plagued by anxieties about lesser things will see in Stein's peace the hand of God.

Surrender in faith grounds us in God and unites us with Jesus. Union with Jesus who suffered, died, and rose again gives us a framework within which to understand our lives. In Jesus, suffering, even totally undeserved suffering, is redeemed. If we intentionally unite our struggles with the life-and-death struggle of Jesus on the Cross, we too are redeemed. Our act of surrender in our time of extreme emptiness allows God's absolute generosity to us to enter in. "That is the gift…the risen Christ…Risen—available, impinging, pressing to come in, held out to us as given."[33] The resurrection of Jesus points the way to the ultimate resolution of all struggles. In Jesus, the paradox of death and resurrection transcends time. In Jesus, dying and rising are one. If we unite ourselves with Jesus at critical times, death becomes life again and again in us.

We are not asked to succumb to the menacing forces that surround us or to evade the vigorous challenges of our lives. We are asked to live through them in confidence, relying on the presence of Jesus within us. From within, Jesus shows us how to struggle and love at the same time. United with his paschal mystery, the balance of our own crisis subtly shifts. We see that even in our most desperate situations we are somehow loved and cared for by God. We recognize that Jesus is willing to go to the point of death again for our sake, out of love. We find the courage to endure our pains in union with his. We realize in the depths of our being that absolutely nothing separates us from God's love for us, shown to us in Jesus.

With tender compassion, Ian Matthew suggests that in the midst of our troubles, we simply "surrender, and be with the One who is content to be with us."[34] If God is willing to be with us in our troubles, unperturbed, maybe we can be too. Logic cannot come near explaining how this happens. Faith and love are the bonds uniting us with Jesus, holding us in the love and mercy of God. What a relief. We can give up our futile efforts to avert or solve the crises of our lives. Grounded in God, we are grounded in love. Nothing else matters.

The stories of C. S. Lewis and Edith Stein told in this chapter exemplify the kind of response we might make when we are in crisis or when we find ourselves unexpectedly in the presence of God. Their lives illustrate the fact that in our lives as well as in theirs, a free choice is available. Likewise, if crisis brings our lives to a halt, we may surrender to God's strength to become able to endure it, because in faith we believe that God is present to us within the crisis itself. Or, we could rely on our own powers to deal with the situation and recklessly hope for the best. Similarly, if God draws near in contemplation, we might surrender to God in faith without completely understanding how God is at work. Or we might shut down in fear.

If we choose in the affirmative toward God as both Lewis and Stein did, that choice may separate us from others. Lewis lost the camaraderie of some of his agnostic colleagues. Stein suffered separation from her beloved mother. Despite the risk and cost involved, surrendering to God in faith unites us with Jesus in a way that provides a context of transcendent meaning for our crises and releases the power of the resurrection within us. After such an act our lives may no longer be our own, but if, as Paul says, we live in Christ, we have nothing to fear.

6
Contemplation

There is a retreat center in New England located on the Atlantic coast. Visitors who go there soon discover an informal daily custom of the house: the silent, reverent anticipation of the dawn. The center sits directly on the ocean, which positions it to capture pristine views of the sunrise each day. The dining room features a wall of floor-to-ceiling windows facing east. An ocean view at any time of day would facilitate meditation, but the early-morning miracle of sunrise there ranks among the best. Those who choose to do so rise while it is still dark and proceed to the dining room where others may have gathered even earlier. The room is dark, no one speaks, there is little movement. Chairs face the direction of the coming dawn. People appear silently in sweatshirts and slippers. Some wrap themselves in afghans, most sip a cup of coffee or tea. First light comes gradually, then a rosy glow, followed by the emergence of the sun's rim. No one moves or does or says anything. They simply allow the day to unfold, without any effort on their part. All of this takes time and occurs without any fuss. When the room fills with daylight, retreatants leave as quietly as they came.

Retreat dedicates an extended period of time to prayer and temporarily suspends all other activity. When we retreat, we deliberately put the rest of our lives on hold. We come before God humbly and simply. We wait upon the Lord. A similar dynamic takes place involuntarily when a crisis occurs. In that case it is the crisis that suspends our regular activity, puts everything else on hold, and requires that we wait. In crisis, we do not know what it is that we await, nor do we see how we could influence the outcome. We assume contemplative attitudes by default. We become silent, we remain still. We are simply, humbly present to the experience. And we wait.

Two well-known figures tell us about contemplative experiences that occurred at decisive junctures in their lives. After more than twenty years of caring for others Gerald May, the psychiatrist and spiritual director mentioned earlier in this study, realized that he himself had reached a critical point. A flash of insight showed him that *he* was the one in need of care, and that an infinite source of love and care awaited him. Similarly, when her own resources were nearly exhausted, Dorothy Day, Catholic peace activist and social justice advocate, accepted the spiritual nurturance offered to her during invaluable days of recollection and retreat. In contemplation both of these highly gifted, exceedingly generous people began to see their lifelong service to others as rooted in and flowing from God's inexhaustible love for them. The change in perspective in turn changed them. Resting in the love and mercy of God, they learned that in caring for others they actually extended to them a love far greater than their own.

Attending

Early on in his psychiatric career, Gerald May discovered the need to recall God's presence as he worked with troubled patients in military and state hospitals and prisons. In fact on good days, when the patients' desperation triggered his own hidden desperation, he could surrender the experience of powerlessness to God right as it occurred. Nevertheless, much later he admits, "Trying to be mindful of love, to practice the presence of God, was the most frustrating thing I ever tried to do." It is only because May so appreciated God's presence that, when he lost track of it, he missed it so acutely. He says, "It was a long time of spiritual suffering…my spiritual failure to be present in love at work seemed like a huge, painful abyss, a gaping wound cut into the middle of every day."[1] Fortunately later, after years of faithful attending to God's presence, the center of gravity in May's spiritual and professional life would shift.

An anonymous British monk writing to a novice about contemplation in the fourteenth century captures some of the same qualities that characterize May's spiritual journey. The younger monk has expressed his frustration with prayer, complaining that the more earnestly he seeks God, the more God seems to withdraw behind an impenetrable cloud. The older monk responds with compassion and tries to identify for the younger monk the value of his patient, consistent, yet seemingly unfulfilled openness toward God. He refers to contemplation as a "blind stirring," an "outstretching," a "naked intent of the will."[2] He reassures the younger monk that his desire for God is, in itself, a very active form of union with God. The urgent desire for God maintains his openness to God and makes it possible for God to enter in.

Chances are that the older monk's reassurance brought only partial relief to the frustrated younger monk. Perhaps the novice would eventually share May's realization: "It is not an easy thing to be mindful of love in the world. It can happen only when our longing catches us like hunger pangs, or when we are given the grace of real presence in the midst of things." May knew from experience that when we attempt most vehemently to find God, God most mysteriously eludes us. He had tried all of the usual techniques to pin God down. He prayed morning and evening, he reminded himself about God during his drive to work. He put notes on his desk and pebbles in his shoes. To his dismay, no effort on his part could compel God to appear.

If we remain faithful in crisis or in contemplation, the apparent absence of God whom we need so desperately extends the limits of our patience and strengthens our resolve. Our souls expand by reaching out to God, like muscles that develop by stretching. That God will come is as certain as the dawn, but when, where, and in what form the divine will manifest itself remains unknown. Like the steadfast servant awaiting his master's return or the wise virgins awaiting the wedding party's arrival, we focus on what we anticipate. What we may not realize is the transforming effect that waiting has on us in the meantime. In May's case, years of faithful attending to God prepared him for a dramatic change in professional careers. Following a long-postponed desire, he terminated his association with psychiatric institutions and began working full-time with Shalem Institute in Washington, DC, an ecumenical Christian community dedicated to the support of contemplative living and leadership.

May had been somewhat involved with Shalem for several years, giving workshops there, facilitating prayer groups, and encouraging others to lead more contemplative lives. Finally he felt that the time had come to make the move from psychiatry to spiritual direction and to see whether the different context of Shalem might bring him into closer contact with God. To his surprise what the new context revealed to him first was the fact that during his years in psychiatric institutions he had gradually developed a thick layer of psychological armor, to defend himself against whatever the day might bring. Looking back at the person he was at that time he says, "I did not know how defended I was until I started working at Shalem. Then, although I kept putting on my armor every day, there was nothing to defend against...It was the weirdest feeling, defending myself against nothing. I think it took more than a year for the habit of armoring myself to stop."

While May was actively searching for God, God was passively preparing him for a whole new approach to life. God drew him to a place where the years of preparation made spiritual sense, and where he could share the lessons of his spiritual journey with other travelers. What is more, he quickly learned that at Shalem his life's work of spiritual direction was being done for him. Rather than assiduously practicing the presence of God, May found himself *in* the presence of God, humbly sharing that sacred presence with others. Years of searching had sharpened his hunger for God and heightened his gratitude for the gift of God's loving care, which he could now see had been there all along.

Recollection

In 1932, in the dark days of the Great Depression, Dorothy Day and Peter Maurin established the foundations of The Catholic Worker, a social justice network and community of people committed to nonviolence, voluntary poverty, and the works of mercy as a way of life. They opened a House of Hospitality in the slums of New York, where many who suffered most from the deprivations of that time had converged. The house offered food, clothing, and temporary shelter to the destitute homeless. The next year they published the first issue of *The Catholic Worker*, a newspaper considered radical then because of its outspoken pacifism and advocacy for society's outcasts. The movement grew rapidly over time, and there are now more than 130 Catholic Worker communities across the United States.

Dorothy Day envisioned none of this at age thirty-five when she and Peter Maurin began their work. In the early days Peter provided the Catholic social justice teachings that guided the mission. His teaching was grounded in the Gospels, the Beatitudes, and the works of mercy. For her part, Dorothy focused intensely on the immediate needs of the poor, and on how she and a community of dedicated volunteers could help them by offering direct service. She solicited donations, set up food and clothing distribution centers, and provided beds for homeless people, often going without food and sleeping on the floor herself. As the Catholic Worker network grew, Peter's health declined and Dorothy found herself increasingly alone at the center of a religious and sociopolitical movement with considerable centrifugal force.

By 1939, when Dorothy was forty-two years old, the work had reached a peak. The newspaper listed over 180,000 subscribers and Houses of Hospitality multiplied. Dorothy held the whole effort together by means of sheer willpower and steadfast determination. However, as the work expanded the drain on her personal and spiritual resources increased proportionately. She could see no end to pressing human needs, and her own efforts to deal with them seemed futile in comparison. It was during this period of near hyperactivity that a friend introduced Dorothy to Father Pacifique Roy, a Josephite priest from Quebec, whose ability to interpret the Gospels provided a spiritual still point in which she could ground herself and her work.

In her autobiography, *The Long Loneliness*, Dorothy describes her first encounter with Father Roy. She says, "We were sitting in the dining room having our morning coffee when he started to talk to us about the love of God. He began with the Sermon on the Mount, holding us spellbound, so glowing was his talk, so heartfelt."[3] The words of this gifted preacher directly addressed the somewhat unrecognized spiritual needs of the struggling Catholic Worker community. Throughout the day volunteers came and went, phones rang, doors slammed, street people sought food and shelter for the night. Father Roy continued to speak with them through it all. In her memoir Dorothy compares the experience to the Emmaus story in which Jesus joins two distraught disciples on the road, explains the Scriptures to them, and goes in with them to share their evening meal. Like the disciples, Dorothy recognized Jesus in the person of this good man.

Sensing their underlying spiritual needs, the Catholic Worker community began to gather for periodic days of recollection during which Father Roy would preach to them and encourage them in their work. They were days of prayer and fasting, opportunities to recenter themselves in the love of God as their source of motivation. Dorothy describes the days of recollection as blessed days. Recalling them nostalgically she says, "After Mass in the morning we had black coffee with no sugar in it and a few slices of bread. At noon we had bread and water. In between we sat and listened to conferences on the love of God…Those were beautiful days. It was as if we were listening to the Gospel for the first time." Stepping aside from their demanding work brought the staff physical rest and relaxation. Immersing themselves in the love of God restored their souls. Dorothy says that during those days, "We saw all things new.

There was a freshness about everything as though we were in love, as indeed we were."[4]

The practice of recollection has deep roots in the spiritual tradition. The anonymous medieval British monk mentioned earlier compares recollection to the habit of putting all of our earthly concerns beneath our feet, under a thick cloud of forgetting so that we may turn our undivided attention toward God. To the same end Ludwig Heyde advises, "One must suspend existential involvement in the world and take time, the time of attention, in which one dwells on what *is*, so that it can show itself *as* it is."[5] To dwell on what is implies dwelling with and in God, present in all things. The practice of recollection operates on the principle that we cannot sustain attention in several different directions at the same time, although many of us consistently strive to do so. In contrast to our often frantic flailing, recollection holds us calmly in one place. John Crosby observes, "The more recollected I am…the more I find myself transcending my environment and indeed in the deepest recollection I find myself opening to God in the center of my being."[6]

It is openness to God that most aptly characterizes the experience of recollection. Recollection sensitizes us to better discern God's constant abiding presence. Times of retreat and recollection may prepare us for contemplation, but they do not and cannot bring contemplation about. Recollection exerts no authority over God or ourselves or the world. It does not dare. Rather it humbly stills and silences us and allows us to realize the presence of God, who is always already there. If and when contemplation occurs, it happens as a pure gift.

Contemplation

Crisis leaves us temporarily suspended, unable to think, feel, or act in the usual ways. Survivors of natural disasters, for example, say that their whole world has been turned upside down by the event, leaving them in an ambiguous state of shock.

CONTEMPLATION

Hurricane Katrina, which swept ruthlessly through the Gulf Coast in September 2005, left thousands of people in this state. One poignant story in the media coverage of the disaster featured several members of the Preservation Hall Jazz Band, one of the inimitable groups of musicians evacuated from New Orleans' legendary French Quarter. In the chaos of the evacuation the musicians had become separated from each other and from their families and homes. Miraculously, within days of the disaster several of them had found their way to New York City, where they were reunited and began to get their bearings.

The reporter who covered the story found them on the empty stage of a New York club, rambling through improvised blues and preparing for a benefit performance to be held that night to raise funds for the hurricane survivors. They had little to say in response to the reporter's questions, preferring to make mournful music together. Finally one of them turned to the reporter and said with cool dignity, "Sir, if and when New Orleans is there again, we'll be there again. Until then, we're here. Right now that's all we've got, but at least we've got that." The reporter could add nothing to the musician's telling words.

Crisis dissolves proud pretensions. Survivors are grateful for whatever little they may have left. Most of all, they are thankful for having survived. If they are fortunate enough to find friends and loved ones, they cling together saying nothing, doing nothing, simply being together and mutually affirming the fact that they are all still there. Although their lives may have been reduced to nearly nothing, they cherish being with each other as an inestimable gift. As the worst of the trauma subsides, the bonds that survivors share help them to begin again.

In her touching book *Too Deep for Words*, Thelma Hall, a Religious of the Cenacle involved in spiritual direction and retreat work, describes contemplation in surprisingly similar terms. "Contemplation is a strange new land," she says, "where everything natural to us seems to be turned upside down, where we learn a new language and a new way of being…where God's seeming absence *is* God's presence, and God's silence *is* God's speech."[7]

The experience does not necessarily feel good. In fact, in contemplation intense feelings fade away. So do lofty thoughts about God, and our vain pride in all that we think we have done for God. Through the love and mercy of God all of that simply disappears. We find ourselves in the presence of God as we are, and we meet God as God truly is. On a very deep level, like the jazz musicians, we cherish just being there.

Two respected sources from the spiritual tradition attempt to describe the same shared state of contemplative presence. In *The Book of Privy Counseling*, a companion treatise to *The Cloud of Unknowing*, the medieval monk gives kindly direction. He says, "In this contemplative work, think of yourself and of God in the same way: that is, with the simple awareness that God is as God is and that you are as you are. In this way your thought will not be fragmented or scattered, but unified in God, who is all."[8] Compared to contemplative presence, all of our thoughts seem fragmented and scattered. It is the presence of God that brings order and peace to all.

The Carmelite tradition offers a comparable description of contemplative presence. In Book II of *The Ascent of Mount Carmel*, John of the Cross provides three classic signs that someone is being drawn to contemplation. His account of the third and final sign tenderly captures the gentle being-together of old friends, dear family, or God and the soul. John says that when in the presence of the beloved such a person likes only to remain in loving awareness, "without particular considerations, in interior peace and quiet and repose." Indeed, he says that the person "prefers to remain only in general, loving awareness...without any particular knowledge or understanding."[9] Nothing that we could think, say, or do could improve upon God's presence. Thinking, speaking, and acting may come later, and they will be immeasurably improved by the experience.

Disasters leave permanent marks on survivors. For many survivors, life becomes infinitely more precious. Relationships and priorities fall into place. Like the psalmist, survivors may find that their hearts are no longer proud, and that they no longer busy themselves with great things. Instead they discover that, as the psalmist says, it is enough to keep one's soul tranquil and quiet, like a child in its mother's arms, as content as a child that has been weaned.[10] Contemplatives use equally consoling metaphors. They speak about interior peace, quiet and repose, about a general loving awareness and a comfortable sort of inertia. They readily admit that they have no particular knowledge or understanding of anything, but that regardless of external circumstances they are sustained by a loving presence that protects them from all harm.

People are changed both by crisis and by contemplation. The changes are as diverse as the people, but there are significant reports from members of both groups that mention positive changes in the way they think and feel. The changes amount to gradual and subtle transformation of these persons, and to a whole new perspective on existence. Humble gratitude for simply *being* becomes a silent accompaniment for their lives.

New Knowing, New Loving

From the safe space of the Shalem Institute, Gerald May looked back at the armored person he had been for so long and reflected that most of the people who knew him then had thought of him as a caring physician. He had even prided himself on being compassionate. Yet he did not know how defended he was until the nurturing, supportive environment of Shalem began to penetrate his encrusted armor. Only then did he realize that he was defending himself against nothing. The non-threatening, nonadversarial context of Shalem allowed May to disarm incrementally. He admits that it took more than a year for the process to run its course. Eventually from an undefended perspective he began to see himself and other people differently. Explaining how the new perspective affected him he acknowledges, "I have but one response to this insight: compassion. I feel the compassion of forgiveness for my own struggles and failures. I could not help it, and I sure did try."[11]

Admitting the apparent shortcomings of his former professional efforts gradually liberated May's spirit and transformed his thinking and feeling about himself and others. The clarity of psychiatric constructs gave way to the ambiguity of companionable relationships. Clinical concern for patients broadened into genuine compassion for colleagues, clients, and friends. Less focused, less analytic ways of thinking ushered in kinder, gentler ways of attending. Over time the calm benevolence of Shalem healed May's mind and heart. In mild self-reproach he says, "I was so caught up in being the helper…that it hardly ever occurred to me that I could be cared for as well. It feels so stupid to think I really felt that way, but it is true."[12] Rather than dwelling on the weaknesses of his former self, May resolved to share the strengths of his new perspective with anyone he might meet who was in similar straits.

May's transformation resulted from a personal and professional crisis in his middle years, but similar changes occur in people who learn to rest in God through contemplative prayer. Commenting on the spiritual wisdom of the author of *The Cloud of Unknowing*, William Johnston outlines two ways of knowing and two ways of loving described there. In both cases the writer holds that contemplation effects the transition from our own ways of knowing and loving to those of God. He teaches that in sharp contrast to the logical, analytical thinking of every day, "a second kind of knowledge takes place at a deeper level of the personality…It is dark, supraconceptual, contemplative, mystical." Likewise, in contrast to a love rooted in the senses, feelings, and emotions, there is "another kind of love that burns at a lower level of the personality in silent tranquility, stretching out toward God whom the contemplative scarcely seems to know."[13]

Contemplation changes us by transforming our two most fundamental capacities: the ability to know and the ability to love. Contemplation moves both capacities to a deeper level within us and simultaneously draws them toward God's transcendent presence beyond us. Because God dwells both intimately within us and infinitely beyond us, God's Spirit must manage the discrepancy. Attempting to do so by our own efforts would indeed be futile. An innate harmony between ourselves and God does exist, but searching for it by force only results in strident discord. All we can do to reduce the spiritual distance is to quiet our thoughts, calm our hearts, and turn our attention toward God. Through these modest, simple gestures, we clear the space necessary for the action of God's Spirit. Our ego-effacing gestures, practiced patiently over time, are the expression of our desire and readiness to be transformed by God.

What might have seemed to May like a professional defeat became a spiritual turning point. Freed from the pressure to objectively categorize his patients' painful sufferings, and released from the obligation to provide them with clinically calculated care, he became a whole new person. The fact that he could look back at his formerly defended self with compassion and forgiveness rather than with scornful disdain gives evidence that the transformation came from God and not from himself. Although in the second half of his life May humbly acknowledged that he "knew" less, he profoundly appreciated being able to love more.

Disappearance of the False Self

In the contemplative literature there are some rather chilling metaphors that intend to convey the effects of spiritual disarming. In endeavoring to express the premise that the individual must decrease so that God may increase, even the most respected spiritual writers resort to phrases like "the shattering of the ego" and the "annihilation of the self." Such vivid metaphors could inadvertently evoke destructive fears in someone who is caught in crisis or who is drawn to contemplative prayer. Providentially, a more homey illustration of the process appears in Gerald May's reflections on the almost imperceptible disappearance of his own false sense of self.

May tells us that he had been away for a week or more giving lectures and workshops to various audiences across the country on behalf of the Shalem Institute. With his medical, psychiatric, and spiritual expertise, he was in great demand on the consulting circuit. He worked generously with interested groups, teaching them, guiding them, and encouraging them to pursue spiritual growth. Nevertheless, when the series of engagements concluded, he was happy to return home and to be welcomed warmly by his wife and children. They talked casually over supper, got caught up on each other's news, and then scattered to do homework or housework or to go out with friends. May describes the evening as being pleasant, yet in some way feeling strange.

Only the next day did he understand the source of his feeling. He realized that on his return home, his family had responded to him lovingly but unexceptionally. To his surprise, he writes, "No one was looking at me as a great authority; not a single person had asked for my wisdom about anything for a whole twenty-four hours! And I was missing it." When he recognized what a relief it was to be taken comfortably for granted by his family, he saw how close he had come to falling into a familiar trap: the need to personify the professional guru. Without intending to, he had brought the aura of learned celebrity home with him. That weighty role threatened his enjoyment of the ordinary family intimacy he so deeply craved. Having learned this lesson earlier, he could quickly shed the mantle of expert and settle into being only Dad. He says, "Thank God that just being at home made me aware of what an ego trip I had begun."[14] Perhaps partly because of the spiritual change that had taken place in him, May relates this story with amused gratitude rather than with feelings of guilt or shame.

Thelma Hall believes that "God loves us too much to leave us in our illusions," and that "sooner or later they will begin to be revealed to us." Whether directly through our prayer or indirectly through our interactions with others, God exposes to us the illusions of the false self. He does so only so that we may energetically dismiss them. Exaggerated autonomy, self-sufficiency, or playing the part of a celebrity—each of these, if left unattended, can become an obstacle between us and God. The purpose of disillusionment, Hall says, is "to undo the dominance of the false self and to center us in the true self: the image and likeness of God within us."[15] We seldom recognize the weight of the false self until we throw it off and then stand free, united with God in our center.

"Pompous images come off in family and abiding friendships," says May, "and the defenses either come down gently on their own or get worn down by attrition."[16] How much more readily we can identify with May's everyday metaphor of the ego wearing down by attrition than the more dramatic metaphors for its violent destruction. While true, the more drastic images tend to instill fear in us, and God's love casts out fear. The touchstone of our spiritual journey is the love and mercy of God, and we know God's love most authentically when our illusions are allowed to evaporate without anyone even noticing. The fact that our mistaken notions are never mentioned exemplifies the infinite tact with which God treats us. As our capacity to accept God's love increases, all other influences decrease, including the whole host of ego illusions we may have had about ourselves. Having put our various personas aside, we find our true selves in God and make abiding with God our true, eternal home.

Centering

For Dorothy Day and the volunteers who became the core of the Catholic Worker movement, days of recollection occasionally grew into longer periods of retreat. Day records her experiences during the first long retreat they made in space offered to them by a group of sisters who ran an orphanage on the outskirts of Pittsburgh. She had been on a speaking trip going from Cleveland to Detroit, then to South Bend, Chicago, and Milwaukee. At each stop she gathered dedicated but exhausted Catholic Worker staff members who went on with her to make the retreat in Pittsburgh. When Dorothy and her group finally arrived at the orphanage, they met other staff members from New York and Baltimore who were waiting for them there.

Day describes them as a mismatched "Bohemian" crowd, who had differences of opinion among themselves about whose poverty was more radical or whose hospitality was more spiritual. One contingent arrived at midnight, and they were drunk. All were dressed poorly and some brought the dirt and smells of the city with them. Indeed, they were a group in need of a retreat, and they threw themselves into the spirit of it with the same reckless ardor they brought to their work. Day recalls, "The five days of complete silence during the retreat were a feast indeed. Every day we had four conferences of an hour each, and after each conference we went to the chapel to pray." The rigorous schedule and the time spent with God gradually took spiritual hold of each one. Day remembers that during those days, God's words spoken through Hosea the prophet came true: "Behold I will allure her and will lead her into the wilderness, and I will speak to her heart."[17] In the desert of the retreat she met God, who gently healed her weary soul. Contentious staff members and urgent social issues paled in comparison with God's presence. The time of retreat reoriented her and renewed the strength and courage she needed for her work. She kept two small notebooks from that retreat that she still enjoyed using for meditation years later.

At this point Day's experience resembles that of someone who has survived a personal crisis, and who has trusted totally in God as the circumstances worked themselves out. The aftermath of the crisis leaves the person silenced and centered in a condition that may be unfamiliar to him: a sort of involuntary retreat. The ordeal through which he has passed has stripped away all falsity and left him open and empty before God, a perfect posture for the divine presence to enter in. Thelma Hall describes the process saying, "It is in the surrender of my false self with its claim of full autonomy, and in letting love become the dynamic central reality of my life, that my true self will be most fully realized."[18] The person who has survived a crisis by blind faith is like the beloved whom God led out to the desert in order to speak to his heart. Having lost many things of lesser value, survivors now know the one thing that is really necessary: the constant, indestructible love of God.

Dorothy Day and the volunteers of the Catholic Worker staff needed the time of retreat to recall the spiritual source of their strength. Some of them had heeded the gospel call to self-giving to such an extent that they feared they had nothing left to give. Their work with the destitute poor who suffered from addictions and handicaps of all sorts had robbed them of any romantic notions they had entertained about lives of service. In Day's own life, the negative social and political repercussions of her activism and the hostile reactions to her editorials in *The Catholic Worker* hit hard. Being unjustly ridiculed, arrested, and even jailed put her on the cross with Jesus continually, but she never flinched. Instead, especially during times of retreat, she relied on the mercy of God and took refuge in God's love. Near the end of her life she could say with calm satisfaction that she had always considered herself richly blessed.

Denys Turner describes the transforming dynamics at work in crisis and contemplation in similar terms. He says, "Faith 'de-centers' us, for it disintegrates the experiential structures of self-hood on which we had centered ourselves, and at the same time draws us into the divine love where we are 're-centered' upon a ground beyond any possibility of experience."[19] The notion of being "de-centered" corresponds with our experience in crisis. Crisis spins the needle of our compass. We lose our confident drivenness and direction. For a time, we do not even know ourselves. What is surprising is that in many cases we will later find that losing our former self was for the best and that the truer, more humble self suits us much better. The true self centered in God, we discover, cannot be shaken.

John Crosby's version of the same dynamic suggests that in realizing our dependence on God, we exchange our illusion of autonomy for a surer state of theonomy, a state of being centered in and directed by God. In theonomy we abdicate our own will for our lives and freely surrender control to God. Crosby says, "We become aware of our personhood in the living encounter with a personal God. To believe that I am known by God, willed by God, called by name, taken seriously…is to have an overwhelming experience of personal selfhood."[20] The person we become when we have encountered God and found God to be infinitely loving far surpasses the person we may previously have tried to be. The person who has clung to God through crisis and found God to be faithful can live without fear. Like Paul, we may appear to others to be broken or defeated, but we possess a supernatural strength.

During days of retreat spent centered in God, Dorothy Day realized that "love is the commandment…It is a choice, a preference. If we love God with our whole hearts, how much heart have we left?"[21] "Little of our own," she would say, "but infinitely more of the heart of God." If we are faithful, we learn through crisis that we can and must rest in the love of God, so that God may love us and eventually love others through us. The startling juxtaposition of our spiritual poverty and of God's unlimited willingness to fulfill us sets the pattern for the rest of our lives.

Still Point

Crisis fixes us in the immediate present. The unknown potential of the crisis holds us in place, silences us, and suspends our ordinary ways of operating. Like the driver of a car sliding on ice, we enter into the experience and await its outcome. Slamming on the brakes only makes things worse, so we go along for the ride and feel we are flying. When the sliding stops and we land in safe space, we sit silently for a while before moving on. Sitting still at that moment is the only response possible.

If our personal crisis emerges out of the multiple transitions of midlife, and if it is extended over a lengthy period of time, we may find ourselves sitting still with some frequency and being somewhat silent about the experience. We appreciate times of respite from the stress, but we do not understand our state. We prefer to forgo explaining ourselves to others. Especially as the intensity of the crisis diminishes and we absorb its implications, we need time to come to terms with ourselves. The crisis may have changed something in us or in our situation. We are not sure what has changed or why. We are not sure about much. Understanding, if it ever comes, is more intuitive than logical and cannot be easily explained. If we have faith, however, we may find new bearings for our lives by spending time silently with God.

Interpreting the spiritual wisdom of *The Book of Privy Counseling*, William Johnston depicts the inner state of someone who has survived a spiritual trial. Like Ignatius, who was vividly aware of evil influences, the author of *Privy Counseling* imagines a soul who has endured an ordeal. No matter how severe the external turmoil has been, he says, "at a deep center of the soul there reigns unruffled calm, a still point of the spirit that is the preserve of God alone."[22] The still point of the spirit rests beyond the range of evil influences. It is grounded in the strength and power of God, impenetrable to their assault. It is a place of impregnable peace. At times by sheer grace contemplation brings us to that still point, and into union with God there.

Dorothy Day and her coworkers treasured their days of retreat as times for contemplative presence to God, away from the constant noise and incessant demands of their urban ministry. "To us retreat was good news," she says. "We made it as often as we could, and refreshed ourselves with days of recollection." So convinced were they of the importance of time spent with God that they dedicated a substantial portion of their meager resources to establishing a retreat house on farmland outside New York City where people could come for spiritual nourishment. Their first farm cost $1,250 for twenty-seven acres, and they quickly outgrew it. "The new farm we purchased for $16,000," Day recalls. "Miraculously, we were given $10,000 by friends to continue our retreat work, all the money coming in within a month from a half dozen of our readers."[23] In their retreat ministry, Day and her dedicated coworkers wanted to share not only their food, clothing, and shelter, but also their spiritual sustenance with others.

Yet the peaceful rural surroundings the farm provided could only invite contemplation; they could not exert pressure on retreatants nor make demands of God. Prayer offered at Maryfarm and other Catholic Worker houses continually surrendered retreatants' lives and fortunes to God. Resting from work and resting in God coincided. Veteran contemplatives tell us that contemplation is always a pure gift, a true grace. It renews and refreshes us in unknown, unseen ways. As one contemplative says in trying to put union with God into words, "I will not deny it, though I cannot explain it."[24] Nor could any person who has ever received this inestimable gift.

Day herself, whom everyone recognized as an indefatigable worker, knew her need for spiritual renewal. Fifteen years into her exhausting ministry, as she neared fifty years of age, she acknowledged the severe limitations of her own personal and spiritual resources. She writes, "It is not only for others that I must have these retreats. It is because I too am hungry and thirsty for the bread of the strong...I too must drink at these good springs so that I may not be an empty cistern and unable to help others."[25] Day's ability to give of herself generously to others for more than eighty years bears eloquent witness to the sustaining effects of her prayer.

The middle years may bring us to an involuntary still point in our lives. They may confound us with questions about what will come next, or how we will manage. Nevertheless, like the timeless moment at the peak of a competitive dive or the breathless pause before the powerful impact of a golfer's swing, the still point is full of potential. Our inability to envision the outcome of our predicament does not lessen our spiritual strength. Vivid awareness of our own weakness does not lessen God's power at work within us. What does become obvious when we come to this point is our complete dependence upon God. In fact, accepting dependence upon God may be the very action that opens our spirit to God.

If this is true, as John Crosby says, "There are rare moments of greatly heightened freedom in which I am able, in a single act, to leap out of despair and to accept myself before God."[26] The choice between despair and hope lies at the heart of each significant crisis in life. The single act of self-acceptance before God, regardless of embarrassing, discouraging, or frustrating life events, unites us with God as we make it. Though the troubles that have brought us to this point may be most disturbing, we suddenly know from experience that there is no greater or more healing intimacy than to be united with God in our deepest center. There is no greater confidence, security, or love.

Indwelling

Later in life, Gerald May speaks with the excitement of one who has stumbled upon an immeasurable treasure. Earnestly he entreats his readers: "Find your heart as best you can, follow it toward the source of love as much as possible, consecrate yourself and trust. God is present, God's love is irrevocable, and you can trust it and trust yourself within it."[27] In the second half of his life it is irrelevant to May that he had spent a large portion of the first half of life trying to make significant things happen. Even though he did in fact amass an array of impressive accomplishments, their importance diminished radically in comparison to the discovery of God's love already present within and around him. Like Paul, May forgets the past and thinks only of the good that is yet to come. In his maturity he knows that nothing can happen that would outweigh the supreme advantage of knowing Jesus, the Lord.

If in moments of contemplation we find our hearts and come to a still point within, we meet God who is present there. Christian tradition refers to God's presence as divine indwelling.

By dwelling within, the Spirit of God heals and transforms us imperceptibly until at some point, as Johnston says, "total activity breaks out, not an activity of this faculty or that, but of the whole being."[28] The total activity that breaks out originates in the power and energy of God. It differs markedly from the frenzied activity that originates in us. If we remain quiet in God's presence, divine activity eventually emerges from the still point within. It sustains us in turmoil and provides for us the personal and spiritual resources we need not only to survive but also to transcend whatever difficulties have beset us.

At the same time that we discover God within us, we find that we are also within God. God's goodness shelters and protects our whole being. We are blessed with a real understanding of what Jesus means when he describes his relationship with his disciples at the Last Supper. In the fifteenth chapter of John's Gospel, Jesus tells them, "Make your home in me as I make mine in you," and urges them repeatedly, "Remain in me." No one who really hears this invitation would consciously refuse. No crisis could ever disrupt the mutual indwelling that God desires to share with us. No matter how chaotic or distressing the circumstances of our lives may be, we can rely on the inexhaustible strength and stability of God.

Periods of reflection allow us to reconnect with the divine presence dwelling within. For this purpose the retreatants described at the beginning of this chapter rose early to spend the first hour of the day in silent contemplation. As another possibility, Thelma Hall recommends that we take time at the end of each day to discern how God was present and active within and around us. "For the truth is that we are immersed in God," she says, "receiving from God life and being and love at every moment, as constantly as the air we breathe throughout our lives."[29] Any time of day is ripe for acknowledging God's loving presence. As a matter of fact, Michael Casey says, "The contemplative act is like stepping out of space and time...When we step outside space-time, we step inside God." Relationship becomes intimacy and intimacy becomes identification, "because our whole being is a participation in the being of God."[30]

Gerald May freely admits that many of his earlier efforts to do good works or to earn God's approval were counterproductive. He recalls feeling chronically frustrated and disappointed, as if he were destined to fail God after all. The midlife career change that grew out of sheer desperation altered his perspective completely. What felt like an admission of defeat became a second chance. At Shalem, May learned that God wanted to do far more in and through him than he could ever have imagined doing for God, and that the strength to do anything at all came directly from God. May wants others to experience the same liberating reality. He advises them to relinquish exaggerated expectations and self-imposed burdens. If they follow his advice, he tells them, "Things will change and you will become more free…Your relationships will change. As you claim more of the truth of your own heart, your attachment to other people will lighten…You will not be able to defend yourself, but you will be protected. You can trust God's love."[31]

It is realistic for May to warn that although we surrender ourselves increasingly to God, we may still be unable to defend ourselves against life's incursions. The human potential for frustration, failure, suffering, and death remains, but our ability to accept and endure these onslaughts deepens. In contemplation, as Casey suggests, we step outside of time and space and step inside God. From within God, all things seem possible, and in God's time all things that seem to be wrong will be made right. Indeed, "the sufferings of this present time are not worth comparing with the glory about to be revealed to us."[32] Contemplatives live in time as if it were eternity. God shares with them the infinite perspective of all-embracing love.

7
Resolution

In December 1967, Thomas Merton reflected movingly on the experience of giving a retreat to a group of fifteen contemplative nuns who came to pray at Gethsemane. Near the end of the retreat he wrote, "The four days have been very moving and I feel completely renewed by them: the best retreat I ever made in my life."[1] Merton could not have known at that time that he was writing these words exactly one year before his tragic death at age fifty-three. His reflection represents gratitude not only for the spiritual gifts of the retreat but also for the peaceful resolution of a significant personal crisis he had undergone during the previous year.

Henri Nouwen's decisive move away from academia and into the L'Arche community of Daybreak at age fifty-four allowed for a similar resolution of major life struggles. After the initial adjustment to living at Daybreak, Nouwen recalled coming to a sense of himself that encompassed previously irreconcilable emotions within him. Because emotional conflict between Nouwen and his father had plagued him throughout his adult life, it was fitting that the image of his father triggered a sense of resolution in him. He wrote, "Recently, on looking into a mirror, I was struck by how much I look like my Dad. Looking at my own features, I suddenly saw the man I had admired as well as criticized, loved as well as feared."[2] Finally, the security and acceptance of the Daybreak community had enabled Nouwen to be reconciled with the image of his father in him along with all of its accompanying contradictions.

By its very nature crisis tends toward resolution. In its simplest form, crisis begins with the disruption of involuntary change. It peaks at some point when we choose either to fight the inevitable change or to surrender to God's presence within it. Following that choice the crisis resolves itself, either for better or for worse, and we acquiesce more or less to the outcome depending upon our willingness and ability to rely on God's presence to sustain us. The experiences of Merton and Nouwen illustrate the positive resolution of significant life crises for each of them. In striking ways they also parallel descriptions of the effects of long-term commitment to contemplative prayer.

As we trace the pattern of resolution in the lives of Merton and Nouwen, we will look for similarities to their experience in the vividly descriptive words of Teresa of Avila. Responding to divine inspiration, Teresa began the Reform of Carmel in her early forties. During the next twenty-seven years, she succeeded in establishing fourteen Reform monasteries and writing under obedience several books that remain spiritual classics more than four hundred years later. Nevertheless, in her final major work, *The Interior Castle*, Teresa recounts neither the formidable obstacles she encountered nor her prodigious accomplishments. Instead she explores her experience of increasing union with God and its subtly transformative effects. The peace of soul with which Teresa writes during times that were phenomenally troublesome for her bears witness to her constant and confident reliance upon God.

Healing

In 1989, six years before he died, Henri Nouwen was critically injured by a passing truck while walking from one L'Arche house to another early in the morning on an icy Toronto highway. He suffered five broken ribs, a ruptured spleen, and massive internal bleeding. Twelve hours later, he was dying. Several miraculous features marked the experience, foremost of which was the fact that he survived and recovered physically. In addition, two other remarkable events bore implicit witness to the sustaining presence of God in the crisis. For one thing, at the height of the medical crisis, Nouwen, ordinarily high strung and prone to anxiety, exhibited profound peace. Then, a week later, he freely initiated a long-postponed reconciliation with his father, who flew from Holland to be at his bedside.[3] Striking as it was, Nouwen's extraordinary physical healing only vaguely symbolized the deeper spiritual and emotional healing that accompanied his traumatic ordeal.

Nouwen's personal problems mirrored his undeniable gifts. Although tremendously popular, he never felt fully loved or accepted. While teaching at the best institutions in America, he resisted their academic culture. Despite rating celebrity status, he sought invisibility by living at L'Arche and serving the severely handicapped. Somehow, helping broken people carry their burdens gradually alleviated his own. Midlife commentator Mark Gerzon might find Nouwen to be a classic case. Gerzon recognizes the interwoven physical, emotional, and spiritual healing that can take place in the second half of life, and he holds that genuine health involves healing our deepest wounds. He says, "To be truly healthy is not just a physical or emotional challenge, but a spiritual one as well."[4] As it did for Nouwen, the challenge of healing may include dealing with emotional rifts within us, which, if left unattended, could undermine the peaceful resolution that we seek.

The same friends who knew Nouwen's hyperactivity all too well attested to his fidelity to prayer. Remaining faithful to God through prayer gathered his otherwise scattered resources. He committed himself to the Eucharist, to the Liturgy of the Hours, and to prayer in quiet. No matter how frantic his schedule or how overloaded his calendar, Nouwen reserved the highest priority for prayer. He realized that the only constant in his life was his relationship with God, and it was only there that he found potential for peace. He returned repeatedly to the presence of God as one returns home.

In the pivotal Fourth Mansion of her *Interior Castle*, Teresa of Avila offers a metaphor for the spiritual healing God offers to wounded souls like Nouwen. She suggests sympathetically that these souls have "walked for days and years with strangers." They may even have lost their way. Meandering has fractured and scattered their faculties, yet God with great love and mercy desires to bring them back. Teresa compares God's summons to a shepherd's whistle, calling back vagrant sheep. The shepherd's whistle is so gentle that they barely hear it, and so powerful that they can hardly resist.[5] Once they recognize God calling them to healing and wholeness, they can do nothing better than to respond. Similarly, Nouwen's consistent return to prayer seems to have been his response to God's persistent summons to him.

Nouwen lived six more years after his dreadful accident. During those years his ever-deepening need for God reflected his desire to cooperate with God's call for healing. Yet rather than slowing down when he regained his strength, he became more active than ever. In September 1995, the community at Daybreak sent him on sabbatical, hoping he would get some much-needed rest. Friends joked that he spent most of his sabbatical on an airplane, and that he had five manuscripts up in the air with him at all times. It had become evident to them that although softened and humbled in his later years, Nouwen could not eradicate the immoderate behavior patterns of a lifetime. Spiritual healing translated only marginally into healthier habits. Jungian writer James Hollis addresses this scenario when he differentiates between healing and curing. People who experience healing, he says, may never be completely cured. Still, when the future direction of their lives becomes clear, the meaning of their past struggles somehow mysteriously appears. Like Nouwen, "one may still suffer greatly," Hollis says, "but one will also experience the meaning which flows from finding one's personal path."[6]

Nouwen's personal path involved a far wider itinerary than most. Inner healing, as it finally materialized, brought greater meaning to his life's journey. If he had begun his priestly ministry with L'Arche, rather than concluding it there, Nouwen may never have gained the spiritual insight into human brokenness that he received in later years. Understanding the suffering of the handicapped people at L'Arche helped him to understand

and to accept his own. Like Jesus, Nouwen united his suffering with theirs and found comfort in the process. The peace that flowed from understanding their suffering affirmed the rightness of his circuitous journey and worked as an instrument of healing for his pains.

The understanding of what led up to a crisis often comes only after the crisis is long past. Earlier Henri Nouwen could not have foreseen the accident that threatened his life, but he did learn later to recognize the compulsive patterns that threatened his peace. As his self-knowledge deepened in maturity, so did the sincerity of his prayer. It is similar for us, if we are faithful. Our faults and weaknesses become ever more obvious to us as we mature, yet they are also the means of deepening our relationship with God. God already knows us better than we know ourselves, and God's love for us does not waver. The very act of presenting our need for healing humbly before God transforms us. Coming to God in humility is the one and only thing that is necessary.

Humility

In April 1966, Thomas Merton was in the hospital for surgery. Merton followers know about his infatuation with a student nurse that began at that time. He captured its onset in his journal: "I got a very friendly and devoted student nurse…In fact, we were getting perhaps too friendly…but her affection was an enormous help in bringing me back to life fast." Merton was fifty-one years old at the time and had been living in a hermitage at some distance from the monastery at Gethsemane. When he found out about the relationship, the abbot, whom Merton describes as being very kind, attributed Merton's vulnerability to the hardships of his solitary state as well as to his trying medical condition. The relationship lasted only a few months and its details are not as important as Merton's response to it once it was discovered. Almost immediately, he wrote, "I have been wrong and foolish in all this. Much as I love M. [he was still using flamboyant language to describe the relationship] I should never have let myself be carried away, or become so utterly imprudent…Well, it is clearly over now." Still, emotional reverberations from the relationship colored the ensuing months. Acute longing mixed with Merton's initial reaction of embarrassment and shame. There were a few phone calls and some conflicted dreams. However, by November he could write, "Each morning I wake up feeling a little freer, just as last May each morning I awoke a little more captivated. I now see how much anguish I suffered, but I could not let go! Now, thank God, I can."[7]

 Early on in her classic *Interior Castle*, Teresa of Avila instructs those who would pursue the spiritual life about the foundational importance of self-knowledge and humility. Although her work describes a grand castle with many rooms, she warns that spiritual people should not stay too long in any room except the first one, the room of self-knowledge. She advises lingering there because the great gift of humility resides in the room of self-knowledge. Ever the lover of metaphor, Teresa compares humility to an ordinary but persistent bumble bee. She writes, "Humility, like the bee in the beehive, is always at work. Without it, everything goes wrong."[8] If Teresa is correct, perhaps we may assume that Merton's lifelong efforts at humility cushioned the effects of the romantic crisis of his later years.

 Virtuous people like Merton make conscious efforts to practice humility, but the softening effects of humility are known to all. Speaking about the repercussions of midlife transitions, one psychologist who is not necessarily prone to religious interpretations says that "apart from shock, confusion, even panic, the fundamental result of the Middle Passage is to be humbled."[9] The imbalances of midlife place many in humbling, if not outright compromising, situations. Merton is not alone in having behaved in ways that strikingly contradicted the preceding twenty-five years of his life. So what can be gleaned from his experience may be valuable for others who are confused in their middle years. Merton's ability to recover from and even to find meaning in his destabilizing episode had roots in his appreciation for humility.

Speaking within a spiritual context, Robert Watson tells us that "the contemplative tradition is very clear about the purpose and inestimable value of the kind of self-knowledge that emerges in the wake of disillusionment. It forms one's character in the virtues of humility and charity."[10] Contemplation shatters our illusions about God and about ourselves. It presents to us layers of reality deeper than we had previously imagined. It disposes us to ask the question, "If God is so much greater than I have ever known, then who am I, in comparison?" Answering that question simultaneously humbles and frees us. In maturity we know both the love and the mercy of God. We learn to forgive the errors and indiscretions of our lives. Like Paul, we forget the past and strain ahead for what is still to come.

Expansion

In September 1968, Merton was preparing for the journey to Bangkok, where he would die prematurely. Among his preparations he mentions nonchalantly, "Today I burned M's letters. Incredible stupidity in 1966! I did not even glance at one of them." The resolution of Merton's emotional crisis had somehow expanded his soul so that he could admit the relationship, but not cling to it. Its memory did not hold him. On the contrary, he had moved to a deeper center. He writes, "I have prayed much more in these days. More and more a sense of being lost without it."[11] Merton's words provide an example of a shift in emphasis that sometimes occurs at midlife. Hollis characterizes the shift as a movement from ego to soul. He believes that the crises we survive take us beyond our youthful demands for ego satisfaction and bring us to rest in more spiritual things. Indeed, he says that in later life emotional needs "go generally unmet, and yet one experiences the meaning of suffering, engagement, and the potential incarnation of one's values in the world."[12] Increased tolerance for unmet needs comes from greater spiritual breadth.

If the negative impact of crisis breaks down some of the youthful ego, its positive effect expands the soul. The ability to live patiently with dissatisfaction signals a generosity of spirit that helps us to put the needs of others before our own. In fact, our own needs seem to recede as a consequence of crisis. Having lost a great deal, we find that we need less. Having relinquished security, we are less vulnerable to fear. In Merton's case, the burning of letters represented real freedom of spirit. The journey to Bangkok symbolically opened the hermetical monk to the rest of the world.

Freedom and openness occur in Teresa of Avila's account of persons who practice the prayer of recollection. She tells us that being with God in recollection expands the soul, and that the "expansion can be verified in the fact that the soul is not as tied down as it was before…but has much more freedom."[13] Teresa compares the recollected soul to a mysterious fountain that is filled to capacity. The more water that flows into the fountain, she says, the larger the fountain becomes. Instead of overflowing, the fountain expands to accommodate the increase. So it is with the soul that is united with God, and so it is with us as the crises of our lives retreat. Vividly aware of our weaknesses, we find unknown strength. Having lost a good deal of control, we find more genuine meaning. To our surprise, we discover that we are better off after the crisis than we were before and that our lives have changed in ways that could not be measured or predicted in advance.

Resolution of crisis allows us to come to terms with contradictions that previously stopped us cold. Our spirit, united with the Spirit of God, encompasses all things. From that perspective we begin to tolerate our dual tendencies to love and hate, hope and fear. We share in God's compassion for us, and we accept God's healing, whole-making love. Uniting our will with God's will helps us to love ourselves with God's love for us. In so doing we become instruments of our own healing. Merton writes from this context in his later years. Remembering some of his heated conflicts with the superiors of the order and the frustration of desiring more solitude while living in a community, he writes, "The profoundest and happiest times in my life have been in and around Gethsemane—and also some of the most terrible."[14] In later life his heart has room for both. Peaceful acceptance grows out of his union with God, whose love embraces all.

Beyond Contradictions

All three figures who are the focus of this chapter—Thomas Merton, Henri Nouwen, and Teresa of Avila—dealt with personal paradox. Merton craved the hermit's life while speaking out nationally on social issues and engaging in a global Christian-Buddhist dialogue about contemplation. Nouwen warmed the hearts of countless people with his speaking and writing while his own heart suffered from brokenness and fear. Teresa reformed monasteries, counseled royalty, and wrote exquisitely while barely escaping the Inquisition and enduring numerous debilitating physical ailments. Together, their lives illustrate the courage and strength necessary for those who would move beyond the limitations of contradictions in the second half of life.

Jesus proposes a vision that transcends contradictions. When the disciples of John the Baptist come and question him about his credentials, Jesus tells them to go back and tell John what they see and hear: the blind see, the lame walk, lepers are cleansed, the deaf hear, the dead are raised to life, and the poor have the gospel preached to them.[15] Jesus' words and actions transcend life's most paralyzing paradoxes. The gospel of Jesus itself contradicts ordinary understandings. Knowing Jesus and living the Gospel places us in a sphere where nothing is taken for granted and all earlier assumptions are up for grabs. The new environment may disorient and confuse us at first, but when it becomes habitual, as it does when we develop a contemplative attitude, we begin to see with Jesus' eyes and we learn to love ourselves and others with Jesus' heart.

One follower of Jesus who survived a life-changing crisis shares his struggle and its ultimate resolution with us. After being knocked off his horse and hearing the voice of God addressing him directly, Paul wanted to reform his life. Yet change came slowly to him and seemed to be radically beyond his own ability to accomplish. His body fought mightily with his soul. Even long after his dramatic conversion, Paul failed to do the things he most wanted to do and continued to do the very things he hated.[16] Paul is not the only one who could not understand his own behavior. The account of his struggles has an uncannily familiar ring. We may imagine, for example, that Merton's naive emotional vulnerability astounded him after his many years of ascetical monastic life. We may assume that after being reconciled with his father, Nouwen marveled at his former unwillingness to forgive. It seems fair to say that a crisis later in life actually opened both men to deeper, more comprehensive union with God.

Midlife interpreters Anne Brennan and Janice Brewi believe that adult maturity entails developing an increased tolerance for contradictions. They write, "Soul making in midlife and the mature years requires a great expansion of the mind and heart. This expansion is built in, and demands one's cooperation for the new growth in personality called for in the second half of life." Their description of midlife soul making combines insights from psychological maturity with words of spiritual wisdom. They show us how the ever-expanding perception of the spirit accommodates the ever-deepening knowledge of ourselves and of the world that comes later in life. They counsel, "In the second half of life you cannot understand the world if you do not understand paradox. As consciousness expands and expands exponentially, we see how mysterious life and all other things really are."[17] Adopting this humble attitude relegates the contradictions and paradoxes of our lives to the realm of mystery, rather than that of frustration and disappointment. Somehow our spiritually expanded consciousness makes them easier to bear.

In later life Teresa of Avila seems to have acquired a capacity for paradox. When she was sixty-two years of age, her confessor commanded her to write the work that became *Interior Castle*. At that time she was in miserable health, Rome had threatened to suppress the Reform, and the Inquisition had confiscated the book of her *Life*. She was in no mood to write about union with God. Nevertheless, in her description of the seventh and final mansion, Teresa arrives at a conviction that she eagerly desires to share with others. Speaking from the mysterious place she refers to as the center of the soul or the spirit, she says, "I do not know how to explain this center. That there are trials and sufferings and that at the same time the soul is in peace is a difficult thing to explain."[18] The close juxtaposition of suffering and peace eludes practical description because it also defies practical reasoning. Only in God can souls suffer and rest at the same time. Only in God can there be chaotic tumult outside and peaceful acceptance within. Abiding with God in love heals all wounds and resolves all difficulties. Without satisfying the rational intellect or feeding the pragmatic ego, the presence of God reconciles all.

After his conversion, Paul envisions a reality in which the weak confound the strong and the foolish shame the wise. Others think of Paul as miserable, but he is always rejoicing. They take him for a pauper, but he knows he has everything. Although he speaks about the concrete experiences of his own life, Paul foresees an eschatological and messianic state of affairs. His vision resembles Isaiah's prophecy of a realm where swords become plowshares and spears become pruning hooks, where the wolf lies down with the lamb and the calf and the lion cub feed together.[19] This is God's loving will for us: a world that is one, whole and complete, where opposites complement rather than polarize, where contradictions and paradoxes resolve themselves in a mystery infinitely larger than any single perspective. It is in this mystery that the contemplative dwells and here that our most daunting crises find their meaning and their truth.

Integration

When Henri Nouwen recognized his resemblance to his father in the image that appeared in the mirror, he reacted with mixed feelings. He confides the fact that he had always admired but also criticized his father, loved as well as feared him. Seeing his father's image reflected in his own image reminded Nouwen of their lifelong history of tension. As a sensitive child, Henri had needed to see his father's love demonstrated visibly and to feel it emotionally. Unfortunately, his father's reserved and highly disciplined nature made it difficult for him to satisfy Henri's needs. After the death of his mother, Henri's father seemed to become even more distant from him. Henri's seminary studies, years of graduate work, and travel to America further separated father and son. Through his adult years and well into midlife the need for his father's love and the perception of his father's withholding of it haunted Henri.

Involuntary resentment fueled Nouwen's ambivalence about his father. As much as Henri loved him, he could not forgive his father for the emotional pain their relationship had caused him. As a pastoral psychologist, Nouwen was well aware of the propensity for adults to suffer from unmet childhood needs, especially the needs associated with their parents. He would have studied and diagnosed in others the problem of projection: expecting in adulthood to have others satisfy childhood needs. Yet he seems to have fallen, however unconsciously, into the same trap. He damaged more than one relationship because he expected from someone attention and affection that they could not give. He sought from others the love he had needed in childhood, love that he felt he had never received. Consequently hurt, frustration, disappointment, and emotional vulnerability undermined Henri's happiness and interfered with some of his most significant relationships.

By the time he arrived at L'Arche, Nouwen had begun to come to terms with the awkward and painful scenario just described. In his deepest center he wanted to relinquish any resentment that he still held against his father, and he wanted to break free from any emotional attachments that carried unnecessary expectations of others. Jungian psychologists call this process the withdrawal of projections, and they value it as a sign of real maturity. They believe that acceptance of ourselves includes admission and acceptance of unmet needs and the integration of needs into our overall image of ourselves. Still, as Kathleen Brehony admits, "The withdrawal of our projections, or what in psychological terminology is called integration, is not an easy or all-in-one process. We do not simply get up one day and withdraw our unconscious projections, just as we do not develop wisdom or individuate in a single step."[20]

The near-fatal impact of Nouwen's fateful collision on the Toronto road dramatically accelerated the difficult process of integration in him. Believing as his doctors had told him that his death was near catapulted him precipitously into an encounter with the eternal God. Remarkably, Sue Mosteller, a L'Arche member who was with him in the hospital, reported that Nouwen showed no fear, and that he was ready to go to God. He only asked her to express his forgiveness to anyone who had hurt him, and to ask forgiveness of anyone he had hurt. "He was just peaceful," she said. "His face was clear and radiant. He was not anguished at all."[21] Undoubtedly the sustaining presence of God at that moment brought a degree of peace Nouwen had seldom known.

By the time his father arrived from Holland a week after the accident, Nouwen's condition had stabilized. He welcomed his father and sister with total openness. It was as if a part of Nouwen actually had died as a result of the accident—the hurt, unforgiving part of him—and as if a new, more freely loving person had survived. A friend who witnessed their reunion said, "Something very big happened when his father went to visit him in the hospital. It had to do with forgiveness. That's when he understood something in the prodigal son parable about becoming the father—the day he let his own father go free."[22] Anyone who has ever extended real forgiveness to another who has hurt them knows that the freedom that comes from forgiveness surpasses by far the hardened security of carrying a grudge. Nouwen's reunion with his father graphically illustrates the principle that with forgiveness comes freedom and with freedom comes peace.

Forgiving his father facilitated integration and healing for Nouwen. It represented the resolution of formerly conflicted emotions in him. It also demonstrated the transcendence of opposites that for some persons follows the resolution of life's crises. Mark Gerzon refers to this mysterious phenomenon as adult metamorphosis. As a symbol of the new life generated by the integration of opposites, he says, "I have found no alternative more compelling than the double helix, the key to life itself. It resembles two intertwined staircases, held together by flexible but strong bonds."[23] The double helix might represent the integration of the internal and the external in one person, the blending of strength and weakness in another, the mixture of desire and satisfaction in a third. As it did for Nouwen, integrating in ourselves any contradictions whose unacknowledged opposition may have precipitated our life's crises holds the key to a whole new life for us.

Transformation

Seven months before he died, Thomas Merton was airborne over the Arizona desert on his way to the Monastery of Christ in the Desert near Albuquerque, New Mexico. The vast, barren expanse beneath him mirrored his own inner state. Contemplating it during the monotonous plane ride he wrote, "I am the utter poverty of God. I am his emptiness, littleness, nothingness, lostness." Upon reading these words we might suspect that Merton was caught in one of his chronic struggles with depression, until discovering Merton's own take on the situation. He concluded his musings matter-of-factly, "When this is understood, my life in his freedom, the self-emptying of God in me is the fullness of grace."[24] Merton's calm acceptance of inner emptiness and poverty and his associating those qualities with greater spiritual freedom manifest the spiritual maturity of his later years. His attitudes typify the gradual transformation that accompanies a life lived in and with God.

Teresa of Avila employs a metaphor taken from nature to describe spiritual transformation: the silkworm. Admitting as she often does that she knows very little about the process, she makes a free interpretation of its metamorphosis. She pictures tiny silkworms nourishing themselves on mulberry leaves, growing fat, spinning cocoons, and coming forth as little butterflies. Only one factor mars the appeal of the otherwise perfect natural phenomenon. In order to undergo its transformation, the silkworm must die.[25] Teresa highlights this alarming fact and compares it with the spiritual death a soul undergoes in being transformed by God. While the potential for transformation attracts her readers, the precondition of dying sobers them as well.

Although unaware that he would die within a month, Merton made the same comparison between death and transformation. On November 24, 1968, he wrote, "The process of maturing can be a mysterious way of dying." Merton had been commenting in his journal about the meaning of a vocation, and working out his understanding that a vocation matures as the person matures. He points out carefully that a vocation carries no compulsion from God, and that the person who feels called by God must still choose God freely. "There has to be a dizzying choice," he says, "a definitive rupture by which the certitude he has gained of being called is torn asunder." [26] Merton may have been thinking of his own recent "rupture," the dizzying romantic crisis that threatened his personal integrity, if not his entire monastic vocation. The memory of his painful deliberate choice to remain faithful may still have been fresh and compelling for him. Reorienting as it eventually was, Merton's crisis and its subsequent resolution had shattered any complacency he may have had about his way of life.

It was not until after his death that most Merton followers became aware of the romantic episode that rudely disrupted the serenity of his long-awaited hermit life. And it was not until his journals from that time period became available that those beyond his inner circle learned Merton's mind on the matter. The journals reveal a humble man capable of extreme honesty with himself. No one needed to spell out for Merton the circumstances that made him vulnerable to the relationship. Nor did he need the abbot's admonition to break it off completely. What did surprise Merton and his friends was the fact that a man so schooled in self-knowledge, so alert to dissipating attachments, could have been so captivated so quickly.

Letting go of the relationship symbolized for Merton an ever-deepening dying to self. Over the years he had conscientiously renounced the benefits that accompany fame and influence. He had conformed to the prescriptions of obedience to the superiors of the order. He had admitted openly to himself and to his confessors his struggle to live a monastic life with the temperament of an artist. Yet after years of renunciation, and perhaps because of that very history, emotional attraction hit him hard. Fortunately, once he recognized it, Merton was able to apply to this challenge all of the spiritual discipline he had cultivated earlier in life. Although he was grievously humbled by the experience at the time, he came to see it later as an opportunity to renew his commitment and to offer himself once again more fully to God.

Far from avoiding the life-or-death option that transformation represents, Teresa addresses it head on. She encourages her readers to abandon anything that separates them from the love of God and urges, "Let it die; let this silkworm die, as it does in completing what it was created to do." Her emphatic directive conveys the inseparable connection between death and life. An old life must die before a new life can begin, and if it is to be transformative, the dying will be very real. In addition, the new life that emerges may seem strangely unfamiliar to us and to others. "The soul doesn't recognize itself," says Teresa.[27] Nor do we recognize ourselves by the benchmarks that previously defined us: status, security, predictability, possessions, comforts of all sorts. They are gone, but to our amazement they are hardly missed. The new life that is given to us surpasses them all.

If we have survived the crises of our lives by relying on the love and mercy of God, and if we have freely died to ourselves in doing so, chances are that we have been transformed in the process. We may not even know, and we will not even care. What matters is that we freely and willingly decrease so that God's presence may gradually increase. As one wise spiritual master observes, "At the end of this path, the soul will be transformed into God by love and will resemble God more than itself."[28] We do not begin to resemble God by trying to do so. We resemble God by being willing to die to all within us that is not God, so that all that is of God within us may be born.

True Self

In a poetic passage in his book, *New Seeds of Contemplation*, Thomas Merton formulates a distinction that has enlightened numerous people who are serious about the spiritual life. He distinguishes between the false self and the true self, the former being driven primarily by the ego and the latter being governed by God. Merton believes that the process of spiritual transformation incrementally diminishes the distance between the two. He also sees shifting the balance from the false self to the true self as a lifelong progression, desired by faithful people but originated and sustained only by God. In fact, Merton recognizes that most people make the transition from false self to true by trial and error, with a good deal of purification in the process.

In the same work, Merton includes the image of a person with "a body of broken bones." This startling image resonates poignantly with people who have endured their share of crises in life. In the aftermath of crisis, even one that has been positively resolved, they feel as if they inhabit a body of broken bones. In the calm that follows they enumerate all that has been lost and recall by what providential care they have been saved. Like survivors of natural disasters or escapees from fatal accidents, they are grateful just to be alive. As the trauma of the experience subsides, they become aware of another layer of gratitude. They are thankful when they realize that enduring the crisis has made them wiser and better than they were before.

This study has been directed to faithful people who have undergone a crisis during their middle years and who have relied on God as the crisis unfolded. While their attention was focused on the crisis, their reliance on God may have had spiritual consequences of which they are only dimly aware. Without any effort on their part they may have been converted from a more superficial or false self to a more authentic spiritual identity in God. Merton alludes to this possibility when he writes, "The secret of my identity is hidden in the love and mercy of God." Crisis strips away falsity and superficiality. It shatters illusions and unmasks pretensions. But the inestimable gift hidden in the crucible of crisis is our identification with the good and loving God. Merton continues, "I cannot hope to find myself anywhere except in God. Ultimately the only way I can be myself is to become identified with God in whom is hidden the reason and fulfillment of my existence."[29] Like other spiritual seekers, Merton continued to pursue his true identity in God throughout his life.

People who have had near-death experiences report a strong conviction that they have returned to fullness of life for a reason. The reason usually includes abundant benevolence toward others. These people have encountered the essential goodness in life and they are eager to share it with anyone who is interested. They have been reborn, and if they are faithful people they may know that they now live their new life with God. Merton, for example, wanted to be a model to others—not a model of perfection, but a model of spiritual freedom. In the final year of his life he wrote, "The best thing I can give to others is to liberate myself from the common delusions and be, for myself and for them, free. Then grace can work in and through me for everyone."[30]

Teresa of Avila would agree that we find our true identity only in God. She expresses her version of spiritual transformation with the metaphor of a wax seal, the kind of seal that dignitaries used at that time to imprint their mark on important documents. Teresa believes that the soul who dwells with God is marked with the seal of God's Spirit. The Spirit of God is imprinted on their own so that the two become one and in time the soul reflects the very image of God. All of this happens by the power of God, and not by any maneuvering on the part of the person. "For indeed the soul does no more in this union than does the wax when another impresses a seal on it," she says. "The wax does not impress the seal upon itself; it is only disposed…by being soft."[31] Perhaps midlife transitions soften those who go through them. If the softening increases their receptivity to God and disposes them to identify more fully with God, then the transition transforms them spiritually as well.

Family photos usually bring smiles to our eyes. Looking at pictures of ourselves from one, two, or three decades earlier reminds us of all that has happened in the intervening years. Seeing ourselves surrounded by family and friends prompts nostalgic memories and moves us to humble gratitude. Our faces and shapes may have changed significantly, but the positive effects of loving relationships remain within us. They are our true legacy because they have made us who we are. Difficulties and struggles of the past diminish in comparison to the underlying goodness we perceive. It was appreciative emotions such as these that came to Henri Nouwen when he thought that death was near. He said to those around him, "I have had a good life and I want you to tell people how grateful I am that they have been so good to me."[32] Proximity to eternity evoked humble gratitude in Nouwen, rather than anxious fear. The best of Henri survived.

The potential for becoming the true self we are meant to be draws us through the crises of midlife and into our mature years. We grow into maturity as we grow into contemplation, by becoming softer, emptier, more open, more receptive. This transition represents a real transformation in us, especially if previously we have been people geared to effort, accomplishment, and external affirmation. The wisdom that comes with spiritual maturity suggests to us how much more satisfying it can be to seek God's affirmation first and foremost, and to allow God to continue to unveil our true self within.

Spiritual Maturity

The Book of Revelation features a spectacular scene in which countless figures dressed in white robes stand before the throne of God giving praise. Awed by the scene an elder asks, "Who are these robed in white, and where have they come from?" The elder is told, "These are they who have come out of the great ordeal."[33] Now, having endured their trials, they stand before the throne of God and serve God night and day. God has saved them. They will never hunger or thirst again, and from this point on God will wipe away all tears from their eyes. The scene offers hope, comfort, and unfathomable security. It represents a transcendent state of affairs that the infinite love of God makes available to all.

In moments of doubt, darkness, and insecurity, we crave resolution such as this. If midlife throws us into crisis, however, and if the crisis spins to full tilt, our desperation may threaten to outweigh our hope for resolution. We may entertain the dangerous alternative of despair. Relying on the love and mercy of God, we resist. At some level we know that the strength to resist comes from God, not from ourselves, for it is at critical moments that we realize our weakness most vividly. Crisis challenges the precarious balance between our weakness and God's strength. In faith, blind to the consequences, we choose to let the power of God prevail. At that point, God takes over and we are allowed to rest.

Resting in God is the domain of the contemplative. It is their zone of comfort and security, their spiritual home. After years of practice, the contemplative would rather not know than know, would rather relinquish than possess. Without knowledge or power, they are at peace in God. The anonymous author of *The Cloud of Unknowing* describes their condition. He writes, "As a person matures in this work of love, they will discover that love governs their demeanor befittingly both within and without. When grace draws someone to contemplation it seems to transfigure them even physically so that...they now appear changed and lovely to behold." Exchanging ego for spirit works this miracle, relying on God rather than on oneself. Those who knew the person previously might not recognize them. "Their whole personality becomes so attractive that good people are honored and delighted to be in their company, strengthened by the sense of God that they radiate."[34] What powerful evidence of God's transforming love.

Because we are human, our interiority interacts constantly with our exteriority. Moments of contemplation may give us glimpses of our spiritual home, but we are still in need of a human home. Henri Nouwen explains that the acceptance of the L'Arche community helped to satisfy this need in him. He writes, "I'm a very restless person but L'Arche became for me the place where I really came home. There's nothing in me that desires to go anywhere else." The ability to stay, to rest, and the disappearance of the impulse to run—these are signs of finding one's true home and of becoming one's true self in God. "I'm still a restless person," Nouwen says, "but in the deeper places of myself I really feel I've found home."[35]

We have traced the pattern of moving through midlife crisis by means of faith in the lives of many people. We have drawn comparisons and discovered similarities between their experiences and those of contemplative writers from various ages. We have used contemplative literature as a support for hope in times of darkness. Examining the reports of crisis in the middle years of several well-known spiritual figures has revealed their common humanity. In all cases we have seen that when people of faith turn to God in their need, they are never refused. They may find themselves in uncharted territory, but they learn to call it home.

The first letter of John observes, "We are God's children now, what we will be has not yet been revealed."[36] Spiritual maturity enables us to await the discovery of who we will become with patience and hope. The person God makes of us in the second half of life may bear little resemblance to the person we made of ourselves in the first. In most cases God's work will be a tremendous improvement. If the crises of midlife have brought us to our knees and into the presence of God, perhaps there is no better place that we could be.

Notes

Chapter 1

1. William Bridges, *The Way of Transition: Embracing Life's Most Difficult Moments* (Cambridge, MA: Perseus Publishing, 2001), 2.
2. Ibid., 59.
3. Ibid., 42.
4. Ibid., 130.
5. John F. Crosby, *The Selfhood of the Human Person* (Washington, DC: The Catholic University of America Press, 1996), 175.
6. Gerald G. May, *Care of Mind, Care of Spirit* (San Francisco: HarperSanFrancisco, 1992), 63.
7. Ibid., 200.
8. Ibid., 125.
9. Kathleen Norris, *Dakota: A Spiritual Biography* (New York: Houghton Mifflin, 1993), 150.
10. Ibid., 110.
11. Ibid., 122.
12. Ibid., 8.
13. Margaret Guenther, *Toward Holy Ground: Spiritual Directions for the Second Half of Life* (Cambridge, MA: Cowley Publications, 1995), 124.
14. Ibid., 127.
15. Ibid.
16. Ibid., 129.
17. 2 Corinthians 4:16.
18. Mark 10:21. See Lorene Hanley Duquin, *They Called Her the Baroness: The Life of Catherine de Hueck Doherty* (New York: Alba House, 1995), 111.
19. Lorene Hanley Duquin, *They Called Her the Baroness*, 296.
20. Catherine de Hueck Doherty, *Fragments of My Life* (Notre Dame, IN: Ave Maria Press, 1979), 148.

21. Constance FitzGerald, "Impasse and Dark Night," in *Women's Spirituality: Resources for Christian Development*, ed. Joann Wolski Conn (New York: Paulist Press, 1996), 411.

22. Ibid., 419.

23. Catherine de Hueck Doherty, *Fragments of My Life*, 152.

24. Lorene Hanley Duquin, *They Called Her the Baroness*, 201.

25. Constance FitzGerald, "Impasse and Dark Night," 413.

26. W. W. Meissner, SJ, *To the Greater Glory of God—A Psychological Study of Ignatian Spirituality* (Milwaukee, WI: Marquette University Press, 1999), 12.

27. Ibid., 75–76.

28. Ibid., 75.

29. Ibid., 27.

30. Gerald G. May, *Addiction and Grace: Love and Spirituality in the Healing of Addictions* (San Francisco: HarperSanFrancisco, 1988), 5.

31. Ibid., 7.

32. Ibid., 8.

33. Denys Turner, *The Darkness of God: Negativity in Christian Mysticism* (Cambridge, England: Cambridge University Press, 1995), 65.

34. Romans 7:15.

35. Walter Conn, *The Desiring Self: Rooting Pastoral Counseling and Spiritual Direction in Self-Transcendence* (New York: Paulist Press, 1998), 71.

36. Gerald G. May, *Addiction and Grace*, 1.

37. Denys Turner, *The Darkness of God*, 55.

Chapter 2

1. Michael Ford, *Wounded Prophet: A Portrait of Henri Nouwen* (New York: Doubleday, 1999), 138.

2. Robert S. Stoudt, "The Midlife Crisis: God's Second Call," *Review for Religious* 54 (1995): 136.

3. Mark Gerzon, *Coming into Our Own: Understanding the Adult Metamorphosis* (New York: Delacorte Press, 1992), 5.

4. James Hollis, *The Middle Passage: From Misery to Meaning in Midlife* (Toronto: Inner City Books, 1993), 16.

5. Michael Ford, *Wounded Prophet*, 155.

NOTES

6. John R. Sachs, *The Christian Vision of Humanity: Basic Christian Anthropology* (Collegeville, MN: Liturgical Press, 1991), 73.

7. Leon Tolstoy, *The Complete Works of Leon Tolstoy: My Confession, My Religion, The Gospel in Brief* (New York: Thomas Crowell Co., 1899), 12.

8. Ibid., 13.

9. Ibid., 14.

10. James Hollis, *Creating a Life: Finding Your Individual Path* (Toronto: Inner City Books, 2001), 86.

11. James Hollis, *The Middle Passage*, 26.

12. David Lonsdale, "In a Dark Night? An Ignatian Approach," *The Way* 41:4 (2002): 371.

13. Luke 9:25.

14. David Lonsdale, "In a Dark Night? An Ignatian Approach," 371.

15. Eugene Peterson, *Under the Unpredictable Plant: An Exploration in Vocational Holiness* (Grand Rapids, MI: Eerdmans Publishing Company, 1992), 1.

16. Ibid., 1.

17. Ibid., 26–27.

18. Margaret Dorgan, "Jesus Christ in Carmelite Prayer," in *Carmelite Prayer: A Tradition for the 21st Century*, ed. Keith Egan (New York: Paulist Press, 2003), 94.

19. Ibid., 95.

20. Thomas Keating, *Crisis of Faith, Crisis of Love* (New York: Continuum, 2002), 13.

21. Eugene Peterson, *Under the Unpredictable Plant*, 1.

22. Margaret Dorgan, "Jesus Christ in Carmelite Prayer," 95.

23. Thomas Keating, *Crisis of Faith, Crisis of Love*, 13.

24. Ibid., 33.

25. James Hollis, *The Middle Passage*, 15.

26. Michael Ford, *Wounded Prophet*, 139.

27. James Hollis, *The Middle Passage*, 39.

28. Kathleen A. Brehony, *Awakening at Midlife: Realizing Your Potential for Growth and Change* (New York: Riverhead Books, 1996), 41.

29. Anne Brennan and Janice Brewi, *Passion for Life: Lifelong Psychological and Spiritual Growth* (New York: Continuum, 1999), 30.

30. James Hollis, *The Middle Passage*, 72.

31. Matthew Kelty, *My Song Is of Mercy* (Kansas City, MO: Sheed and Ward, 1994), 7.

32. Ibid., 8.
33. Ibid., 9.
34. Robert S. Stoudt, "The Midlife Crisis: God's Second Call," *Review for Religious* 54 (1995): 131–42, at 137.
35. Ibid.
36. John F. Crosby, *The Selfhood of the Human Person*, 162.
37. Mark Gerzon, *Coming into Our Own*, 92.
38. Kathleen A. Brehony, *Awakening at Midlife*, 132.
39. Matthew Kelty, *My Song Is of Mercy*, 9.
40. William James, *The Varieties of Religious Experience* (New York: Penguin Books, 1958), 73.
41. Robert S. Stoudt, "The Midlife Crisis: God's Second Call," 132.
42. Ibid., 139.
43. William James, *The Varieties of Religious Experience*, 73.
44. Ibid., 74.

Chapter 3

1. Brigitte-Volaine Aufauvre, "Depression and Spiritual Desolation," *The Way* 42, no. 3 (July 2003): 50–51.
2. Kevin Culligan, "The Dark Night and Depression," in *Carmelite Prayer: A Tradition for the 21st Century*, ed. Keith Egan (New York: Paulist Press, 2003), 128.
3. Ibid., 129.
4. Ibid.
5. Denys Turner, *The Darkness of God: Negativity in Christian Mysticism*, 229.
6. James Hollis, *The Middle Passage*, 33.
7. Brigitte-Volaine Aufauvre, "Depression and Spiritual Desolation," 50.
8. John H. Coe, "Musings on the Dark Night of the Soul: Insights from St. John of the Cross on a Developmental Spirituality," in *Spiritual Formation: Counseling and Psychotherapy*, eds. Todd Hall and Mark McGinn (New York: Nova Science Publishers, 2003), 71–91.
9. Charles J. Healy, SJ, *Christian Spirituality: An Introduction to the Heritage* (New York: Alba House, 1999), 248.
10. Charles J. Healy, SJ, *Christian Spirituality*, 248. These descriptions are paraphrased from David L. Fleming, SJ, in *Draw Me Into Your*

NOTES

Friendship: The Spiritual Exercises, a Literal Translation and a Contemporary Reading (St. Louis, MO: The Institute of Jesuit Sources, 1996), 250–251. Consolation and desolation are defined in numbers 316 and 317 of *The Spiritual Exercises*.

11. Brigitte-Volaine Aufauvre, "Depression and Spiritual Desolation," 48–49.

12. David Lonsdale, "In a Dark Night? An Ignatian Approach" *The Way* 41, no. 4 (2002): 372.

13. Ibid.

14. Jules Toner, SJ, *A Commentary on St. Ignatius' Rules for the Discernment of Spirits* (St. Louis, MO: The Institute of Jesuit Sources, 1982), 274.

15. W. W. Meissner, SJ, *To the Greater Glory of God*, 259–260.

16. David Lonsdale, "In a Dark Night? An Ignatian Approach," 376. For Ignatius' own words on the matter, see David L. Fleming, SJ, *Draw Me Into Your Friendship*, 248–253. The strategies are outlined in numbers 318 to 321 of *The Spiritual Exercises*.

17. W. W. Meissner, SJ, *To the Greater Glory of God*, 262. See number 319 of *The Spiritual Exercises*.

18. Ibid., 286.

19. Kieran Kavanaugh and Otilio Rodriguez, *The Collected Works of St. John of the Cross* (Washington, DC: ICS Publications, 1973), 22.

20. Ibid., 33.

21. Kevin Culligan, "The Dark Night and Depression," 124–125.

22. Michael O'Connor, "Spiritual Dark Night and Psychological Depression: Some Comparisons and Considerations," *Counseling and Values* 46, no. 2 (January 2002): 139.

23. Ruth Burrows, *Ascent to Love: Spiritual Teaching of St. John of the Cross* (London: Sheed and Ward, 2000), 107–108.

24. Kieran Kavanaugh, *John of the Cross: Doctor of Light and Love* (New York: Crossroad, 1999), 40–41.

25. Kevin Culligan, "The Dark Night and Depression," 126.

26. Colin Thompson, *St. John of the Cross: Songs in the Night* (Washington, DC: Catholic University of America Press 2003), 187.

27. Michael O'Connor, "Spiritual Dark Night and Psychological Depression," 144.

28. John H. Coe, "Musings on the Dark Night of the Soul," 74.

29. Michael O'Connor, "Spiritual Dark Night and Psychological Depression," 144.

30. Gerald May, *Care of Mind, Care of Spirit*, 105.
31. David Lonsdale, "In a Dark Night? An Ignatian Approach," 373–374. See also John H. Coe, "Musings on the Dark Night of the Soul," 89.
32. Jules Toner, SJ, *A Commentary on St. Ignatius' Rules for the Discernment of Spirits*, 271, 275.
33. John H. Coe, "Musings on the Dark Night of the Soul," 89.
34. Michael O'Connor, "Spiritual Dark Night and Psychological Depression," 142.
35. Jules Toner, SJ, *A Commentary on St. Ignatius' Rules for the Discernment of Spirits*, 281.

Chapter 4

1. Sue Monk Kidd, *When the Heart Waits: Spiritual Direction for Life's Sacred Questions* (New York: HarperCollins, 1992), 4–5, 16.
2. Margaret Silf, *Inner Compass: An Invitation to Ignatian Spirituality* (Chicago: Loyola Press, 1999), 26–28.
3. Denys Turner, *The Darkness of God*, 247.
4. Sue Monk Kidd, *When the Heart Waits*, 162.
5. Margaret Silf, *Inner Compass*, xviii.
6. John H. Coe, "Musings on the Dark Night of the Soul," 85.
7. Sue Monk Kidd, *When the Heart Waits*, 164.
8. Margaret Dorgan, "Jesus Christ in Carmelite Prayer," 93.
9. Thomas Keating, *Crisis of Faith, Crisis of Love*, 37.
10. Margaret Silf, *Inner Compass*, 30–31.
11. Sue Monk Kidd, *When the Heart Waits*, 94.
12. Ian Matthew, *The Impact of God: Soundings from St. John of the Cross* (London: Hodder and Staughton, 1995), 82.
13. Colin Thompson, *St. John of the Cross: Songs in the Night* (Washington, DC: Catholic University of America Press, 2003), 220.
14. Ruth Burrows, *Ascent to Love*, 34.
15. Patrick Hart and Jonathan Montaldo, eds., *The Intimate Merton: His Life from His Journals* (New York: HarperCollins, 1999), 187.
16. Ibid., 206–207.
17. Ibid., 188.

NOTES

18. Sandra Cronk, *Dark Night Journey, Inward Re-patterning Toward a Life Centered in God* (Wallingford, PA: Pendle Hill Publications, 2001), 73.

19. Patrick Hart and Jonathan Montaldo, eds., *The Intimate Merton*, 187–188.

20. Michael Casey, *Toward God: The Ancient Wisdom of Western Prayer* (New York: HarperCollins, 1996), p. 153.

21. Patrick Hart and Jonathan Montaldo, eds., *The Intimate Merton*, 201.

22. Ibid.

23. William H. Shannon, *Silence on Fire: Prayer of Awareness* (New York: Crossroad, 2000), 23.

24. Ibid., 21.

25. Mark Gerzon, *Coming into Our Own*, 113–114.

26. Thomas Keating, *Crisis of Faith, Crisis of Love*, 22.

27. Patrick Hart and Jonathan Montaldo, eds., *The Intimate Merton*, 233.

28. Cardinal Joseph Bernardin, *The Gift of Peace* (New York: Image Books, 1998), 51.

29. Vilma Seelaus, "Transformation and Divine Union in the Carmelite Tradition," in *Carmelite Prayer: A Tradition for the 21st Century*, ed. Keith Egan (New York: Paulist Press, 2003), 149.

30. Margaret Guenther, *Toward Holy Ground*, 108.

31. Ludwig Heyde, *The Weight of Finitude, On the Philosophical Question of God* (New York: SUNY Press, 1999), p. 40.

32. Margaret Guenther, *Toward Holy Ground*, 124.

33. James Hollis, *Creating a Life*, 80.

34. Cardinal Joseph Bernardin, *The Gift of Peace*, 136.

35. Ibid., 151.

36. William H. Shannon, *Silence on Fire*, 5.

37. John R. Sachs, *The Christian Vision of Humanity: Basic Christian Anthropology* (Collegeville, MN: Liturgical Press, 1991), 75–76.

Chapter 5

1. C. S. Lewis, *Surprised by Joy: The Shape of My Early Life* (New York: Harcourt Brace, 1955), 224.

2. John F. Crosby, *The Selfhood of the Human Person*, 271.

3. Ruth Burrows, *Ascent to Love*, 43.
4. Michael Casey, *Toward God*, 167.
5. Ruth Burrows, *Ascent to Love*, 111.
6. Ibid., 57.
7. C. S. Lewis, *Surprised by Joy*, 227.
8. James Hollis, *Creating a Life*, 80.
9. Ludwig Heyde, *The Weight of Finitude*, 119.
10. C. S. Lewis, *Surprised by Joy*, 229.
11. Ibid., 227.
12. Ludwig Heyde, *The Weight of Finitude*, 125.
13. C. S. Lewis, *Surprised by Joy*, 227.
14. Ruth Burrows, *Ascent to Love*, 100.
15. R. A. Herrera, *Silent Music: The Life, Work and Thought of St. John of the Cross* (Grand Rapids, MI: W. B. Eerdmans, 2004), 78, 80.
16. Vilma Seelaus, "Transformation and Divine Union in the Carmelite Tradition," 141.
17. C. S. Lewis, *Surprised by Joy*, 228.
18. Wiltraud Herbstrith, *Edith Stein: A Biography* (San Francisco: Ignatius Press, 1985), 49–50.
19. Ibid., 51.
20. Ibid., 65.
21. James Hollis, *The Middle Passage*, 113.
22. Michael O'Connor, "Spiritual Dark Night and Psychological Depression," 145.
23. Vilma Seelaus, "Transformation and Divine Union in the Carmelite Tradition," 149.
24. Anne Brennan and Janice Brewi, *Passion for Life*, 50.
25. Wiltraud Herbstrith, *Edith Stein*, 70.
26. Ibid., 71.
27. Ibid., 72.
28. Ibid., 122.
29. James Hollis, *Creating a Life*, 46.
30. Ian Matthew, *The Impact of God*, 130, 133.
31. Michael Casey, *Toward God*, 155.
32. Wiltraud Herbstrith, *Edith Stein*, 167.
33. Ian Matthew, *The Impact of God*, 125.
34. Ibid., 147.

NOTES

Chapter 6

1. Gerald May, *The Awakened Heart: Living Beyond Addiction* (San Francisco: HarperSanFrancisco, 1991), 213–216, for here and the next two pages.
2. William Johnston, *The Mysticism of the Cloud of Unknowing* (New York: Fordham University Press, 2000), 98.
3. Dorothy Day, *The Long Loneliness: An Autobiography* (New York: Harper and Row, 1952), 246.
4. Ibid., 250–251.
5. Ludwig Heyde, *The Weight of Finitude*, 34.
6. John F. Crosby, *The Selfhood of the Human Person*, 170.
7. Thelma Hall, *Too Deep for Words: Rediscovering* Lectio Divina (New York: Paulist Press, 1988), 49. (I have substituted the word *God* for the word *he* in the text.)
8. William Johnston, ed., *The Cloud of Unknowing and The Book of Privy Counseling* (New York: Doubleday, 1973), 150. (Again, I have substituted the word *God* for the word *he* in the text.)
9. Kieran Kavanaugh and Otilio Rodriguez, *The Collected Works of St. John of the Cross*, 141.
10. Psalm 131:2.
11. Gerald May, *The Awakened Heart*, 217.
12. Ibid., 219.
13. William Johnston, *The Mysticism of the Cloud of Unknowing*, 89–90, 97–98.
14. Gerald May, *The Awakened Heart*, 222.
15. Thelma Hall, *Too Deep for Words*, 42.
16. Gerald May, *The Awakened Heart*, 222.
17. Dorothy Day, *The Long Loneliness*, 255.
18. Thelma Hall, *Too Deep for Words*, 22.
19. Denys Turner, *The Darkness of God*, 251.
20. John F. Crosby, *The Selfhood of the Human Person*, 301.
21. Dorothy Day, *The Long Loneliness*, 256–257.
22. William Johnston, *The Mysticism of the Cloud of Unknowing*, 174.
23. Dorothy Day, *The Long Loneliness*, 259, 262.
24. Ian Matthew, *The Impact of God*, 22.
25. Dorothy Day, *The Long Loneliness*, 263.
26. John F. Crosby, *The Selfhood of the Human Person*, 271.
27. Gerald May, *The Awakened Heart*, 244.

28. William Johnston, *The Mysticism of the Cloud of Unknowing*, 234.
29. Thelma Hall, *Too Deep for Words*, 54.
30. Michael Casey, *Toward God*, 168.
31. Gerald May, *The Awakened Heart*, 245.
32. Romans 8:18.

Chapter 7

1. Patrick Hart and Jonathan Montaldo, eds., *The Intimate Merton*, 317.
2. Michael Ford, *Wounded Prophet*, 174.
3. Ibid., 176–177.
4. Mark Gerzon, *Coming into Our Own*, 53.
5. Teresa of Avila, *The Interior Castle*, trans. Kieran Kavanaugh and Otilio Rodriguez (New York: Paulist Press, 1979), 77–78.
6. James Hollis, *Creating a Life*, 101.
7. Patrick Hart and Jonathan Montaldo, eds., *The Intimate Merton*, 275, 288, 303–304.
8. Teresa of Avila, *The Interior Castle*, 42–43.
9. James Hollis, *The Middle Passage*, 41.
10. Robert A. Watson, "Toward a Union in Love: The Contemplative Spiritual Tradition and Contemporary Psychoanalytic Theory in the Formation of Persons," in *Spiritual Formation: Counseling and Psychotherapy*, eds. Todd Hall and Mark McGinn (New York: Nova Science Publishers, 2003), 61.
11. Patrick Hart and Jonathan Montaldo, eds., *The Intimate Merton*, 336.
12. James Hollis, *Creating a Life*, 94.
13. Teresa of Avila, *The Interior Castle*, 81–82.
14. Patrick Hart and Jonathan Montaldo, eds., *The Intimate Merton*, 235.
15. Matthew 11:5.
16. Romans 7:15–24.
17. Anne Brennan, and Janice Brewi, *Passion for Life*, 44, 79.
18. Teresa of Avila, *The Interior Castle*, 182.
19. 1 Corinthians 1:27–30; 2 Corinthians 6:10; Isaiah 2:4; 11:6–7.
20. Kathleen Brehony, *Awakening at Midlife*, 164.
21. Michael Ford, *Wounded Prophet*, 177.

NOTES

22. Ibid.

23. Mark Gerzon, *Coming into Our Own*, 124–125.

24. Patrick Hart and Jonathan Montaldo, eds., *The Intimate Merton*, 328.

25. Teresa of Avila, *The Interior Castle*, 91.

26. Patrick Hart and Jonathan Montaldo, eds., *The Intimate Merton*, 360.

27. Teresa of Avila, *The Interior Castle*, 93.

28. R. A. Herrera, *Silent Music*, 79.

29. Thomas Merton, *New Seeds of Contemplation* (Norfolk, CT: New Directions, 1961), 34–36. (I have substituted the word *God* for the masculine pronoun.)

30. Patrick Hart and Jonathan Montaldo, eds., *The Intimate Merton*, 333.

31. Teresa of Avila, *The Interior Castle*, 96.

32. Michael Ford, *Wounded Prophet*, 177.

33. Revelation 7:13–15. The whole scene is described in verses 9–17.

34. William Johnston, *The Mysticism of the Cloud of Unknowing*, 117. (I have substituted inclusive pronouns in this passage.)

35. Michael Ford, *Wounded Prophet*, 187.

36. 1 John 3:2.

Bibliography

Aufauvre, Brigitte-Volaine. "Depression and Spiritual Desolation." *The Way*, 42 (2003): 47–56.

Bernardin, Joseph Cardinal. *The Gift of Peace*. New York: Image Books, 1998.

Brehony, Kathleen A. *Awakening at Midlife: Realizing Your Potential for Growth and Change*. New York: Riverhead Books, 1996.

Brennan, Anne, and Janice Brewi. *Passion for Life: Lifelong Psychological and Spiritual Growth*. New York: Continuum, 1999.

Bridges, William. *The Way of Transition: Embracing Life's Most Difficult Moments*. Cambridge, MA: Perseus Publishing, 2001.

Burrows, Ruth. *Ascent to Love: Spiritual Teaching of St. John of the Cross*. London: Sheed and Ward, 2000.

Casey, Michael. *Toward God: The Ancient Wisdom of Western Prayer*. New York: HarperCollins, 1996.

Coe, John H. "Musings on the Dark Night of the Soul: Insights from St. John of the Cross on a Developmental Spirituality." In *Spiritual Formation: Counseling and Psychotherapy*, edited by Todd Hall and Mark McGinn, 71–91. New York: Nova Science Publishers, 2003.

Connor, Charles P. *Classic Catholic Converts*. San Francisco: Ignatius Press, 2001.

Cronk, Sandra. *Dark Night Journey: Inward Re-patterning Toward a Life Centered in God*. Wallingford, PA: Pendle Hill Publications, 2001.

Crosby, John F. *The Selfhood of the Human Person*. Washington, DC: The Catholic University of America Press, 1996.

Culligan, Kevin G. "The Dark Night and Depression." In *Carmelite Prayer: A Tradition for the 21st Century*, edited by Keith Egan, 119–138. New York: Paulist Press, 2003.

Cunningham, Agnes. "The Dark Night of the Soul—When Only Hope Remains." *Chicago Studies*, 33:111–123 (August 1994).

Day, Dorothy. *The Long Loneliness: An Autobiography*. New York: Harper and Row, 1952.

BIBLIOGRAPHY

DeCaussade, Jean-Pierre. *The Sacrament of the Present Moment*. New York: HarperCollins, 1989.

Doherty, Catherine de Hueck. *Fragments of My Life*. Notre Dame, IN: Ave Maria Press, 1979.

Dorgan, Margaret. "Jesus Christ in Carmelite Prayer." In *Carmelite Prayer: A Tradition for the 21st Century*, edited by Keith Egan, 82–100. New York: Paulist Press, 2003.

Dubay, Thomas. *The Fire Within: St. Teresa of Avila, St. John of the Cross and the Gospel—On Prayer*. San Francisco: Ignatius Press, 1989.

Duquin, Lorene Hanley. *They Called Her the Baroness: The Life of Catherine de Hueck Doherty*. New York: Alba House, 1995.

Egan, Keith, ed. *Carmelite Prayer: A Tradition for the 21st Century*. New York: Paulist Press, 2003.

———. "The Solitude of Carmelite Prayer." In *Carmelite Prayer, A Tradition for the 21st Century*, edited by Keith Egan, 39–62. New York: Paulist Press, 2003.

Finley, James. *The Contemplative Heart*. Notre Dame, IN: Sorin Books, 2000.

FitzGerald, Constance. "Impasse and Dark Night." In *Women's Spirituality: Resources for Christian Development*, edited by Joann Wolski Conn, 410–435. New York: Paulist Press, 1996.

Fleming, SJ, David L. *Draw Me into Your Friendship: The Spiritual Exercises, a Literal Translation and a Contemporary Reading*. St. Louis, MO: The Institute of Jesuit Sources, 1996.

Ford, Michael. *Wounded Prophet: A Portrait of Henri Nouwen*. New York: Doubleday, 1999.

Fowler, James. *Stages of Faith*. New York: HarperCollins, 1995.

Gerzon, Mark. *Coming into Our Own: Understanding the Adult Metamorphosis*. New York: Delacorte Press, 1992.

Guenther, Margaret. *Toward Holy Ground: Spiritual Directions for the Second Half of Life*. Cambridge, MA: Cowley Publications, 1995.

Hall, Thelma. *Too Deep for Words: Rediscovering Lectio Divina*. New York: Paulist Press, 1988.

Hall, Todd, and Mark McMinn, eds. *Spiritual Formation: Counseling and Psychotherapy*. New York: Nova Science Publishers, 2003.

Harris, Jan. *Quiet in His Presence: Experiencing God's Love through Silent Prayer*. Grand Rapids, MI: Baker Books, 2003.

Hart, Patrick, and Jonathan Montaldo, eds. *The Intimate Merton: His Life from His Journals*. New York: HarperCollins, 1999.

Healy, SJ, Charles J. *Christian Spirituality: An Introduction to the Heritage*. New York: Alba House, 1999.

Herbstrith, Waltraud. *Edith Stein: A Biography*. San Francisco: Ignatius Press, 1985.

Herrera, R. A. *Silent Music: The Life, Work and Thought of St. John of the Cross*. Grand Rapids, MI: W. B. Eerdmans, 2004.

Heyde, Ludwig. *The Weight of Finitude: On the Philosophical Question of God*. New York: SUNY Press, 1999.

Hollis, James. *Creating a Life: Finding Your Individual Path*. Toronto: Inner City Books, 2001.

———. *The Middle Passage: From Misery to Meaning in Midlife*. Toronto: Inner City Books, 1993.

James, William. *The Varieties of Religious Experience*. New York: Penguin Books, 1958.

Jantzen, Grace. *Julian of Norwich*. Mahwah, NJ: Paulist Press, 1987.

Johnston, William. *The Mysticism of the Cloud of Unknowing*. New York: Fordham University Press, 2000.

———, ed. *The Cloud of Unknowing and The Book of Privy Counseling*. New York: Doubleday, 1973.

Julian of Norwich. *Julian of Norwich, Showings*. Translated by Edmund Colledge, OSA, and James Walsh, SJ. New York: Paulist Press, 1978.

Kavanaugh, Kieran. "Contemplation and the Stream of Consciousness." In *Carmelite Prayer: A Tradition for the 21st Century*, edited by Keith Egan, 101–118. New York: Paulist Press, 2003.

———. *John of the Cross: Doctor of Light and Love*. New York: Crossroad, 1999.

——— and Otilio Rodriguez. *The Collected Works of St. John of the Cross*. Washington, DC: ICS Publications, 1973.

Keating, Thomas. *Crisis of Faith, Crisis of Love*. New York: Continuum, 2002.

Kelty, Matthew. *My Song Is of Mercy*. Kansas City, MO: Sheed and Ward, 1994.

Kidd, Sue Monk. *When the Heart Waits: Spiritual Direction for Life's Sacred Questions*. New York: HarperCollins, 1992.

BIBLIOGRAPHY

Lewis, C. S. *Surprised by Joy: The Shape of My Early Life*. New York: Harcourt Brace, 1955.

Lonsdale, David. *Eyes to See, Ears to Hear: An Introduction to Ignatian Spirituality*. Maryknoll, New York: Orbis Books, 2000.

―――. "In a Dark Night? An Ignatian Approach." *The Way*, 41(2002): 371–381.

Matthew, Ian. *The Impact of God: Soundings from St. John of the Cross*. London: Hodder and Staughton, 1995.

May, Gerald. *Addiction and Grace*. San Francisco: HarperSanFrancisco, 1991.

―――. *Care of Mind, Care of Spirit*. San Francisco: HarperSanFrancisco, 1992.

―――. *The Awakened Heart: Living Beyond Addiction*. San Francisco: HarperSanFrancisco, 1991.

―――. *The Dark Night of the Soul: A Psychiatrist Explores the Connection Between Darkness and Spiritual Growth*. San Francisco: HarperSanFrancisco, 2003.

McBride, J. Le Bron. *Spiritual Crisis: Surviving Trauma to the Soul*. New York: Haworth Pastoral Press, 1998.

Meissner, SJ, W. W. *To the Greater Glory of God—A Psychological Study of Ignatian Spirituality*. Milwaukee, WI: Marquette University Press, 1999.

Merton, Thomas. *Contemplative Prayer*. New York: Image Books, 1996.

―――. *New Seeds of Contemplation*. Norfolk, CT: New Directions, 1961.

―――. *The Inner Experience: Notes on Contemplation*. Edited by William H. Shannon. San Francisco: HarperSanFrancisco, 2003.

Norris, Kathleen. *Dakota: A Spiritual Biography*. New York: Houghton Mifflin, 1993.

Nouwen, Henri. *Sabbatical Journey: The Diary of His Final Year*. New York: The Crossroad Publishing Co., 1998.

Oben, Freda Mary. *Edith Stein: Scholar, Feminist, Saint*. New York: Alba House, 1998.

O'Connell, Marvin. *Blaise Pascal: Reasons of the Heart*. Grand Rapids, MI: Eerdmans, 1997.

O'Connor, Michael. "Spiritual Dark Night and Psychological Depression: Some Comparisons and Considerations." *Counseling and Values*, 46 (2002): 137–148.

Palmer, Parker J. *The Courage to Teach: Exploring the Inner Landscape of a Teacher's Life*. San Francisco: Jossey-Bass, 1998.

Pennington, Basil. *True Self/False Self*. New York: Crossroad, 2000.

Peterson, Eugene. *Under the Unpredictable Plant: An Exploration in Vocational Holiness*. Grand Rapids, MI: Eerdmans Publishing Company, 1992.

Robinson, John C. *Death of a Hero, Birth of the Soul*. Tulsa, OK: Council Oak Books, 1997.

Rolheiser, Ronald. *The Shattered Lantern: Rediscovering a Felt Presence of God*. New York: Crossroad, 2001.

Sachs, John R. *The Christian Vision of Humanity: Basic Christian Anthropology*. Collegeville, MN: Liturgical Press, 1991.

Seelaus, Vilma. "Transformation and Divine Union in the Carmelite Tradition." In *Carmelite Prayer: A Tradition for the 21st Century*, edited by Keith Egan, 139–164. New York: Paulist Press, 2003.

Shannon, William H. *Silence on Fire: Prayer of Awareness*. New York: Crossroad, 2000.

Sharp, Joseph. *Spiritual Maturity: Stories and Reflections for the Ongoing Journey of the Spirit*. New York: Berkeley Publishing Group, 2001.

Silf, Margaret. *Inner Compass: An Invitation to Ignatian Spirituality*. Chicago: Loyola Press, 1999.

Snowdon, David. *Aging with Grace: What the Nun Study Teaches Us About Leading Longer, Healthier and More Meaningful Lives*. New York: Bantam Books, 2001.

Stoudt, Robert S. "The Midlife Crisis: God's Second Call." *Review for Religious*, 54 (1995): 131–142.

Teresa of Avila. *The Interior Castle*. Translated by Kieran Kavanaugh and Otilio Rodriguez. New York: Paulist Press, 1979.

Thompson, Colin. *St. John of the Cross: Songs in the Night*. Washington, DC: Catholic University of America Press, 2003.

Tolstoy, Leon. *The Complete Works of Leon Tolstoy: My Confession, My Religion, The Gospel in Brief*. New York: Thomas Crowell Co., 1899.

Toner, SJ, Jules. *A Commentary on St. Ignatius' Rules for the Discernment of Spirits*. St. Louis, MO: Institute of Jesuit Sources, 1982.

Turner, Denys. *The Darkness of God: Negativity in Christian Mysticism*. Cambridge: Cambridge University Press, 2002.

Vaillant, George. *Aging Well: Surprising Guideposts to a Happier Life from the Landmark Harvard Study of Adult Development*. Boston: Little, Brown and Co., 2002.

BIBLIOGRAPHY

Watson, Robert A. "Toward Union in Love: The Contemplative Spiritual Tradition and Contemporary Psychoanalytic Theory in the Formation of Persons." In *Spiritual Formation: Counseling and Psychotherapy*, edited by Todd Hall and Mark McGinn, 53–79. New York: Nova Science Publishers, 2003.